Cross-Stitch Florals

Marie Barber

Sterling Publishing Co., Inc. New York
A Sterling/Chapelle Book

Chapelle Ltd.

Owner
Jo Packham

Editor
Karmen Quinney

Graphic Artist
Susan Jorgensen

Staff
Ann Bear, Areta Bingham,
Kass Burchett, Marilyn Goff,
Holly Hollingsworth, Barbara Milburn,
Linda Orton, Leslie Ridenour,
Cindy Stoeckl, Gina Swapp, Sara Toliver

Photographer
Kevin Dilley/Hazen Photography Studio

Library of Congress Cataloging-in-Publication Data

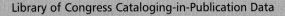

10 9 8 7 6 5 4 3 2 1

Published by Sterling Publishing Company, Inc.,
387 Park Avenue South, New York, NY 10016
© 2001 by Chapelle Limited
Distributed in Canada by Sterling Publishing
% Canadian Manda Group, One Atlantic Avenue, Suite 105
Toronto, Ontario, Canada M6K 3E7
Distributed in Great Britain and Europe by Cassell PLC
Wellington House, 125 Strand, London WC2R 0BB, England
Distributed in Australia by Capricorn Link (Australia) Pty
Ltd.
P.O. Box 6651, Baulkham Hills, Business Centre, NSW 2153,
Australia
Printed in USA
All Rights Reserved

Sterling ISBN 0-8069-1997-3

If you have any questions or comments, please contact:
Chapelle Ltd., Inc., P. O. Box 9252 Ogden, UT 84409
(801) 621-2777 • FAX (801) 621-2788 • e-mail: chapelle@
chapelleltd.com • website: www.chapelleltd.com

Table of Contents

About the Author

Marie Barber, born and raised in Kristianstad, Sweden, now lives in Ragland, Alabama, on the Coosa River with her husband and their three children.

Marie says she has always loved to draw and illustrate. At the age of 14, she was the youngest student to study oil painting under the instruction of the late Dr. Göran Trönnberg.

She came to the United States in 1983 as an exchange student, and in 1987, returned after being accepted to the Art Institute of Atlanta. She has freelanced as a novel illustrator for a Swedish weekly publication and her artwork is featured at Loretta Goodwin's Gallery in Birmingham, Alabama. Although she has explored several avenues of the art world, Marie says she found her passion in 1993 when she began designing cross-stitch patterns.

General Instructions

Introduction

Contained in this book are over 555 floral cross-stitch designs.

Each double-page spread of graphed designs has its own color code. To create one-of-a-kind motifs, vary colors in graphed designs.

Cross-stitch Items to Know

Fabric for Cross-stitch

Counted cross-stitch is worked on even-weave fabrics. These fabrics are manufactured specifically for counted-thread embroidery, and are woven with the same number of vertical as horizontal threads per inch.

Because the number of threads in the fabric is equal in each direction, each stitch will be the same size. The number of threads per inch in even-weave fabrics determines the size of a finished design.

Number of Strands

The number of strands used per stitch varies, depending on the fabric used. Generally, the rule to follow for cross-stitching is three strands on Aida 11, two strands on Aida 14, one or two strands on Aida 18 (depending on desired thickness of stitches), and one strand on Hardanger 22.

For backstitching, use one strand on all fabrics. When completing a French Knot (FK), use two strands and one wrap on all fabrics, unless otherwise directed.

Finished Design Size

To determine the size of the finished design, divide the stitch count by the number of threads per inch of fabric. When a design is stitched over two threads, divide stitch count by half the threads per inch. For example, if a design with a stitch count of 120 width and 250 height was stitched on a 28 count linen (over two threads making it 14 count), the finished size would be 8⅝" x 17⅞".

$$120 \div 14" = 8⅝" \text{ (width)}$$

$$250 \div 14" = 17⅞" \text{ (height)}$$

$$\text{Finished size} = 8⅝" \times 17⅞"$$

Preparing Fabric

Cut fabric at least 3" larger on all sides than the finished design size to ensure enough space for desired assembly. To prevent fraying, whipstitch or machine-zigzag along the raw edges or apply liquid fray preventive.

Needles for Cross-stitch

Blunt needles should slip easily through the fabric holes without piercing fabric threads. For fabric with 11 or fewer threads per inch, use a tapestry needle #24; for 14 threads per inch, use a tapestry needle #24, #26, or #28; for 18 or more threads per inch, use a tapestry needle #26 or #28. Avoid leaving the needle in the design area of the fabric. It may leave rust or a permanent impression on the fabric.

Floss

All numbers and color names on the codes represent the DMC brand of floss. Use 18" lengths of floss. For best coverage, separate the strands and dampen with a wet sponge, then put together the number of strands required for the fabric used.

Centering Design on Fabric

Fold the fabric in half horizontally, then vertically. Place a pin in the intersection to mark the center. Locate the center of the design on the graph. Begin stitching all designs at the center point of the graph and fabric.

Securing Floss

Insert needle up from the underside of the fabric at starting point. Hold 1" of thread behind the fabric and stitch over it, securing with the first few stitches. To finish thread, run under four or more stitches on the back of the design. Avoid knotting floss, unless working on clothing.

Another method of securing floss is the waste knot. Knot floss and insert needle down from the right top side of the fabric about 1" from design area. Work several stitches over the thread to secure. Cut off the knot later.

Carrying Floss

To carry floss, run floss under the previously worked stitches on the back. Do not carry thread across any fabric that is not or will not be stitched. Loose threads, especially dark ones, will show through the fabric.

Cleaning Finished Design

When stitching is finished, soak the fabric in cold water with a mild soap for five to ten minutes. Rinse well and roll in a towel to remove excess water. Do not wring. Place the piece face down on a dry towel and iron on a warm setting until the fabric is dry.

Stitching Techniques

Backstitch (BS)

1. Insert needle up between woven threads at A.

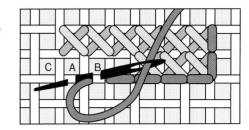

2. Go down at B, one opening to the right.

3. Come up at C.

4. Go down at A, one opening to the right.

Bead Attachment (BD)

1. Make first half of a cross-stitch.

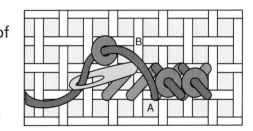

2. Insert needle up between woven threads at A.

3. Thread one bead before going down at B, the opening diagonally across from A.

4. To strengthen stitch, come up again at A and either go through bead again or split threads to lay around bead and go down at B again.

Cross-stitch (XS)

Stitches are done in a row or, if necessary, one at a time in an area.

1. Insert needle up between woven threads at A.

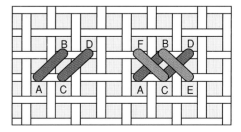

2. Go down at B, the opening diagonally across from A.

3. Come up at C and go down at D, etc.

4. To complete the top stitches, creating an "X", come up at E and go down at B, come up at C and go down at F, etc. All top stitches should lie in the same direction.

Eyelet Stitch (ES)

1. Insert needle up between woven threads at A.

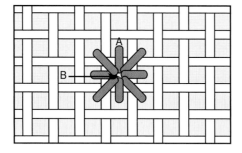

2. Go down at B (center). Continue around center eight times, bringing needle down through center each time.

French Knot (FK)

1. Insert needle up between woven threads at A, using one strand of embroidery floss.

2. Loosely wrap floss once around one needle.

3. Go down at B, the opening across from A. Pull floss taut as needle is pushed down through fabric.

4. Carry floss across back of work between knots.

Lazy Daisy Stitch (LD)

1. Insert needle up between woven threads at A.

2. Go down at B, using same opening as A.

3. Come up at C, crossing under two threads. Pull through, holding floss under needle to form loop.

4. Go down at D, crossing one thread.

Long Stitch (LS)

1. Insert needle up between woven threads at A.

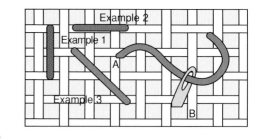

2. Go down at B, crossing two threads. Lay flat. Repeat A–B for each stitch. Stitch may be horizontal, vertical, or diagonal as indicated in examples 1, 2, and 3. The length of the stitch should be the same as the length indicated on the graph.

Satin Stitch (SS)

1. Insert needle up between woven threads at A.

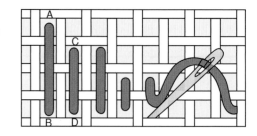

2. Go down at B, forming a straight stitch.

3. Come up at C and go down at D, forming another smooth straight stitch.

4. Repeat to fill design area.

Tent Stitch (TS)

Stitches are done in a row horizontally or vertically from the left to the right.

1. Insert needle up between woven threads at A.

2. Go down at B, the opening diagonally across from A.

3. Come up at C and down at D, etc.

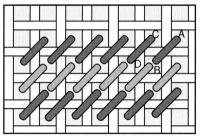

Horizontal Tent Stitch

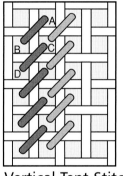

Vertical Tent Stitch

Treasure Attachment (TR/AW)

1. Make first half of a cross-stitch.

2. Insert needle up between woven threads at A.

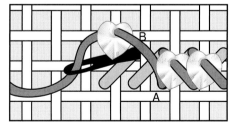

3. Thread one treasure before going down at B, the opening diagonally across from A.

4. To strengthen stitch, come up again at A and either go through bead again or split threads to lay around bead and go down at B again.

European Fields page 106

Wrapped Backstitch (WBS)

1. Make a row of backstitches slightly longer than usual.

2. Insert needle up at A, weave over and under the backstitches from one direction without piercing the fabric.

3. Repeat to fill desired area.

Botanical Africa

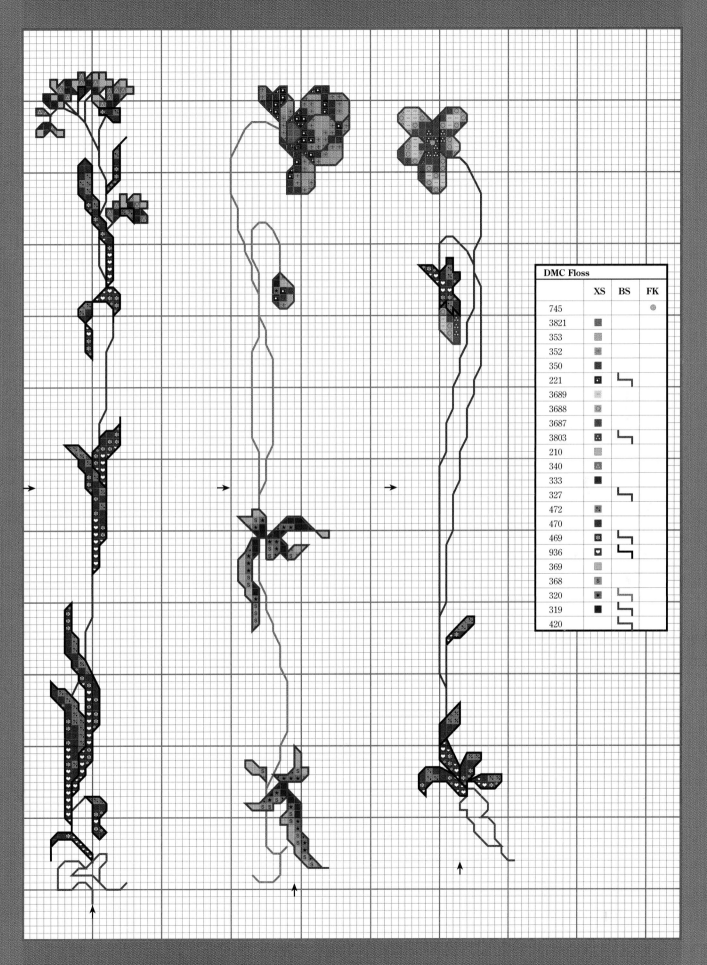

DMC Floss			
	XS	**BS**	**FK**
745			◉
3821	▦		
353	▦		
352	▦		
350	▦		
221	▣	⌐	
3689	⊟		
3688	◉		
3687	▦		
3803	▣	⌐	
210	▦		
340	△		
333	▦		
327		⌐	
472	▦		
470	▦		
469	✾	⌐	
936	♡	⌐	
369	▦		
368	Ⓢ		
320	★	⌐	
319	■	⌐	
420		⌐	

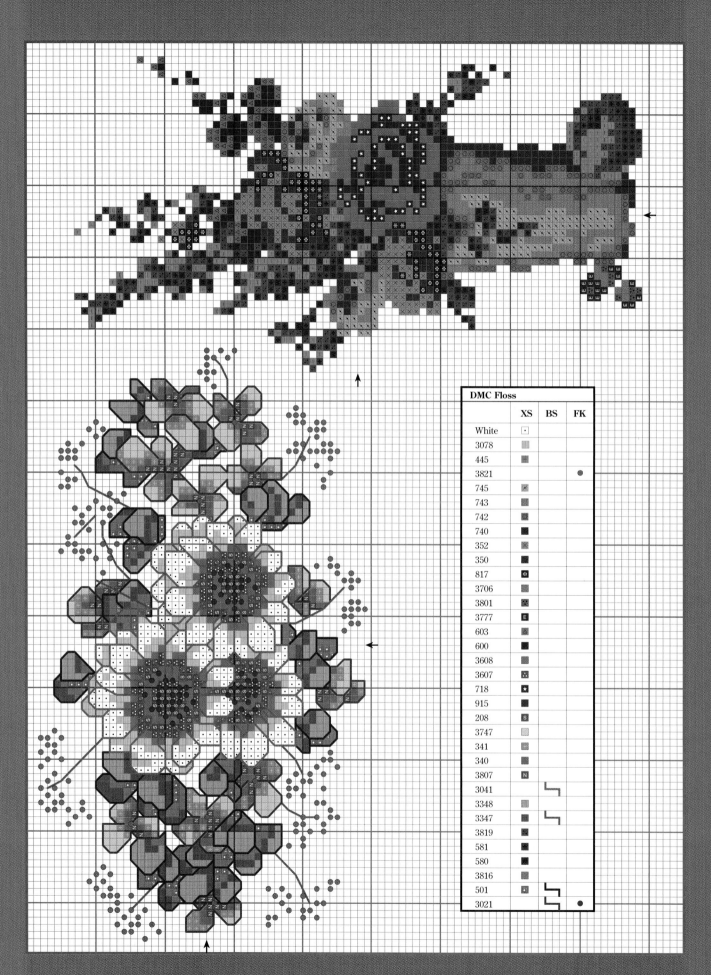

DMC Floss				
	XS	BS	FK	LS
712				
676				
3829	N			
761				
760				
3722				
221				
3687			●	
3685		⌐	●	
327			●	
*Evergreen or DMC 3052		⌐		/
3364				
3363	A			
3362	M	⌐		
834			●	
422				
420				
613				
612				
611				
3031		⌐	●	
*Caron Collection Waterlillies				

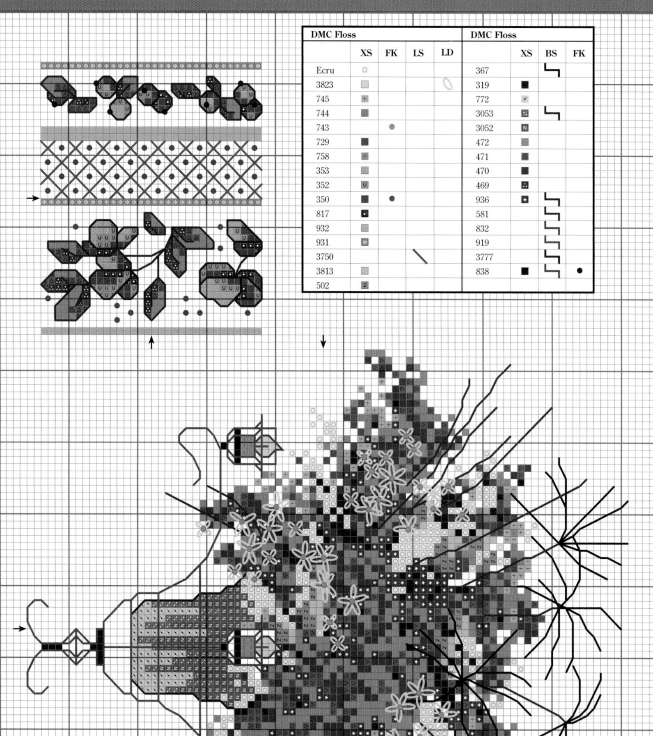

DMC Floss						DMC Floss			
	XS	FK	LS	LD			XS	BS	FK
Ecru	○					367			
3823				⬭		319	■		
745	⊞					772			
744						3053	▨		
743		●				3052	N		
729	■					472			
758						471	▦		
353						470	■		
352	U					469	▨		
350	■	●				936	✳		
817	▣					581			
932						832			
931	✳					919			
3750			/			3777			
3813						838	■		●
502	Z								

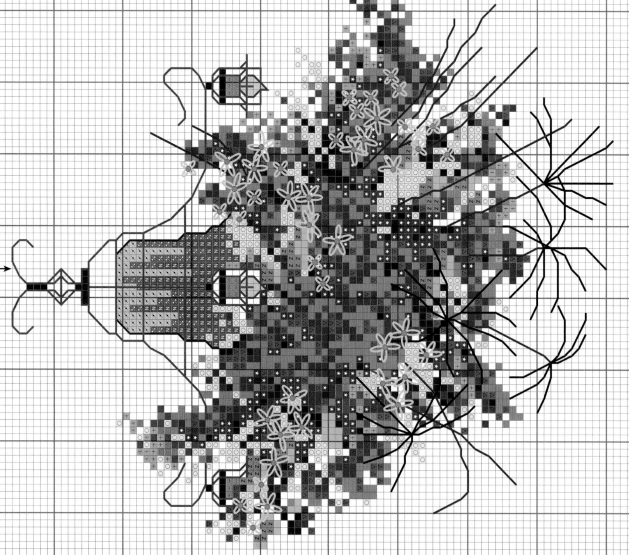

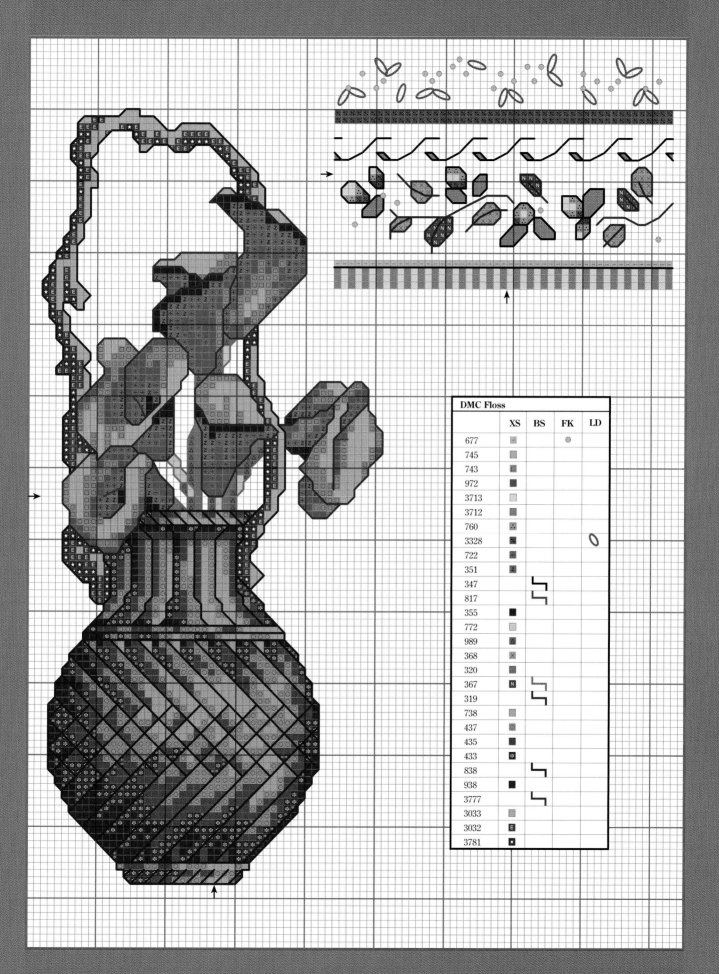

DMC Floss				
	XS	BS	FK	LD
677			●	
745				
743				
972				
3713				
3712				
760				
3328				O
722				
351	Z			
347		⌐		
817				
355	■			
772				
989	▲			
368	✕			
320				
367	N	⌐		
319				
738				
437				
435				
433				
838		⌐		
938	■			
3777		⌐		
3033				
3032	E			
3781	★			

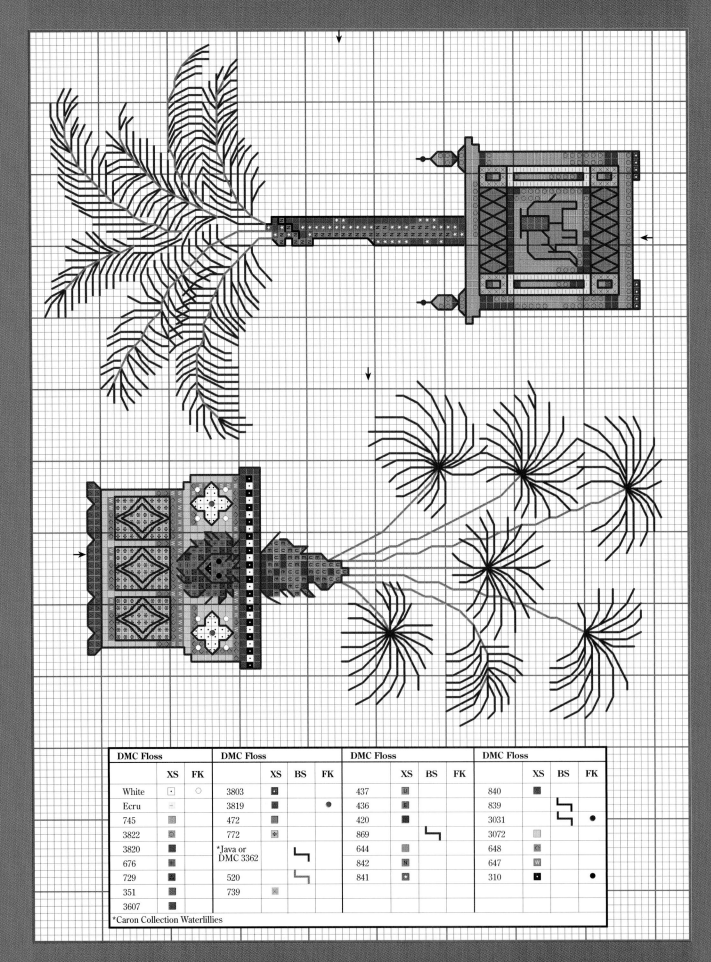

DMC Floss			DMC Floss				DMC Floss				DMC Floss		
	XS	FK		XS	BS	FK		XS	BS	FK		XS	BS	FK
White	·	○	3803				437	U			840			
Ecru			3819			●	436	E			839			●
745			472				420				3031			●
3822			772				869				3072			
3820			*Java or DMC 3362				644				648			
676							842	N			647	W		
729			520				841				310	■		●
351			739											
3607														
*Caron Collection Waterlillies														

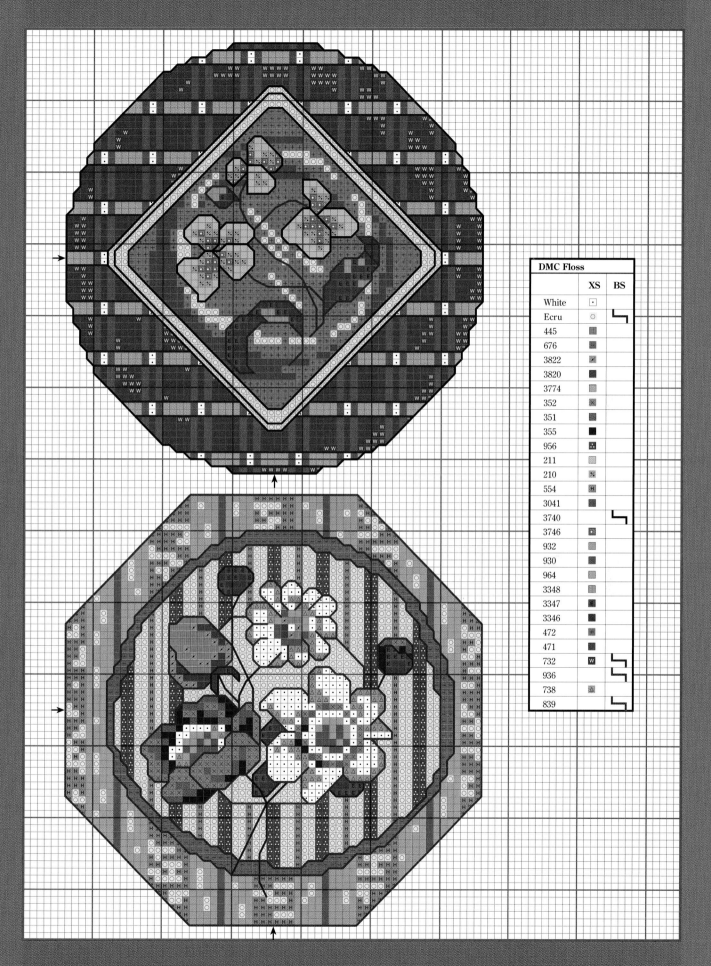

DMC Floss		
	XS	**BS**
White	·	
Ecru	○	⌐
445		
676		
3822		
3820		
3774		
352		
351		
355		
956		
211		
210		
554	H	
3041		
3740		⌐
3746		
932		
930		
964		
3348		
3347		
3346		
472		
471		
732	W	⌐
936		⌐
738	▲	
839		⌐

DMC Floss		
	XS	BS
White	·	
*Lemon-lime or DMC 727		
3046 } **014C		
3779	H	
352	+	
351		
3777		
3688		
3687		
211		
210	H	
209		
3740		⌐
747		
3761		
519		
3811	X	
3814		
992	U	
562		
368		
734		
733		
732		
472		
3051	★	⌐
869		⌐

*Caron Collection Waterlillies

**Kreinik Cord

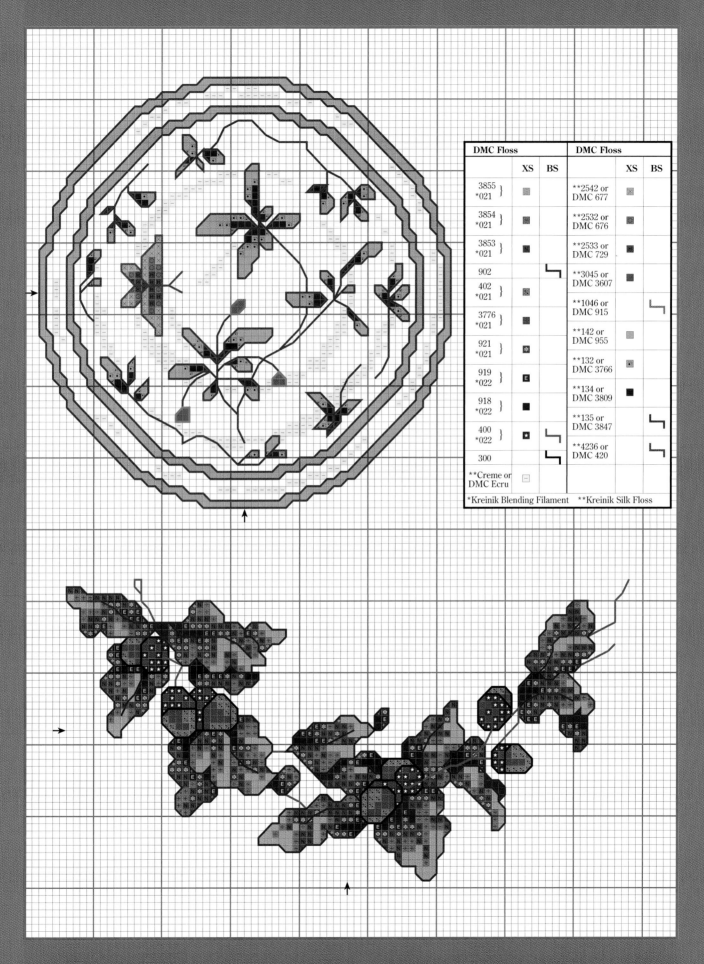

DMC Floss	XS	BS	DMC Floss	XS	BS
3855 *021 }	▦		**2542 or DMC 677	▦	
3854 *021 }	▦		**2532 or DMC 676	▦	
3853 *021 }	N		**2533 or DMC 729	▦	
902		⌐	**3045 or DMC 3607	▦	
402 *021 }	▦		**1046 or DMC 915		⌐
3776 *021 }	▦		**142 or DMC 955	▦	
921 *021 }	▦		**132 or DMC 3766	▦	
919 *022 }	E		**134 or DMC 3809	■	
918 *022 }	■		**135 or DMC 3847		⌐
400 *022 }	★	⌐	**4236 or DMC 420		⌐
300		⌐			
**Creme or DMC Ecru	⊡				

*Kreinik Blending Filament **Kreinik Silk Floss

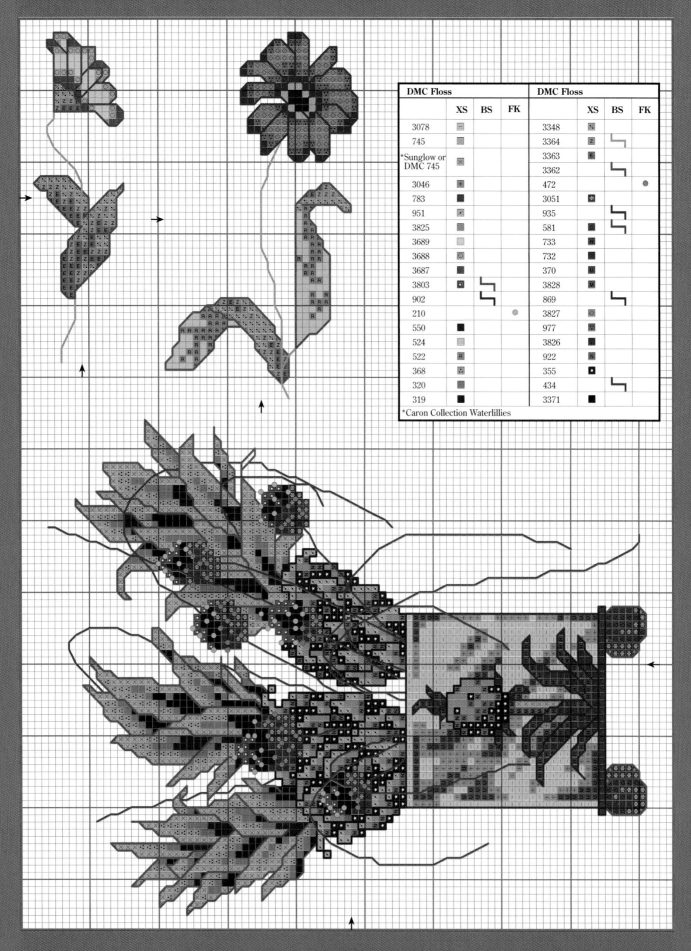

DMC Floss					DMC Floss			
	XS	BS	FK			XS	BS	FK
3078					3348			
745					3364			
*Sunglow or DMC 745					3363			
					3362			
3046					472			●
783					3051			
951					935			
3825					581			
3689					733			
3688					732			
3687					370			
3803					3828			
902					869			
210			●		3827			
550					977			
524					3826			
522					922			
368					355			
320					434			
319					3371			

*Caron Collection Waterlillies

18

DMC Floss			
	XS	BS	FK
White	·		
745			
743			
727			
725			
3822			
3820		⌐	
729			
780		⌐	
3607			●
209			
800			
799			
798			
820			
472			
471			
470			
937			
936	E		
934		⌐	
989			
987	M	⌐	
436			
977			
976		⌐	
3826			
975			
300		⌐	
310	■	⌐	●

DMC Floss			
	XS	BS	LS
White	·		
3078			
745			
726			
3047	⊠		
211			
210	◎		
472			
471			
470	Z		
469			
936		⌐	
833	F		
612	U		
611			
610	✳		
3021		⌐	
*2246 or DMC 780		⌐	
*3423 or DMC 524	⊡		
*2111 or DMC 772			
*2142 or DMC 472	⊡		
*2123 or DMC 471	W		╱
*2124 or DMC 470	H		
*2125 or DMC 469		⌐	
*2126 or DMC 937		⌐	
*2136 or DMC 935	★		
*1844 or DMC 934		⌐	
*2242 or DMC 437	△		
*Kreinik Silk			

DMC Floss		
	XS	**BS**
Ecru	⊟	
3774	▦	
3743	▨	
3042	◉	
471	▩	
470		⌐
3348	▨	
3347	⊡	
3346	E	
3345	▪	
895		⌐
402	⊞	
3776	▦	
400	▪	
3866	⊠	
613	▨	
612	M	
611	▦	
3031		⌐
3024	△	
310	▪	⌐

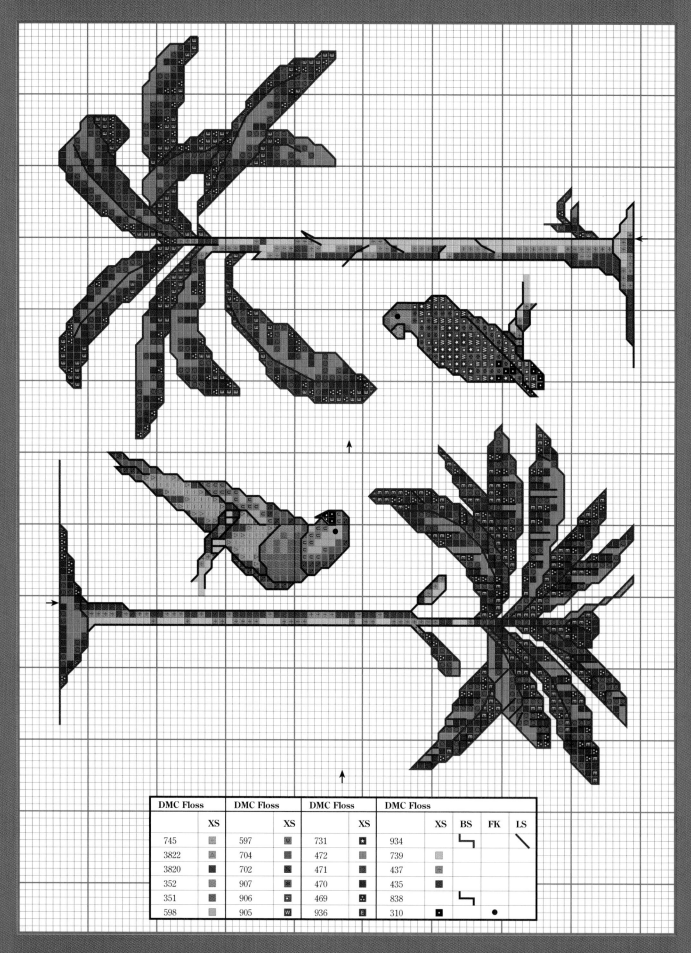

DMC Floss		DMC Floss		DMC Floss		DMC Floss		BS	FK	LS
	XS		XS		XS		XS			
745		597		731		934				
3822		704		472		739				
3820		702		471		437				
352		907		470		435				
351		906		469		838				
598		905		936		310				

DMC Floss		
	XS	**BS**
Ecru	⊟	
3774	▨	
3743	▦	
3042	◉	
471	▦	
470		⌐
3348	▦	
3347	◪	
3346	E	
3345	▪	
895		⌐
402	⊞	
3776	▦	
400	▪	
3866	⊠	
613	▦	
612	M	
611	▦	⌐
3031		⌐
3024	▲	
310	▪	⌐

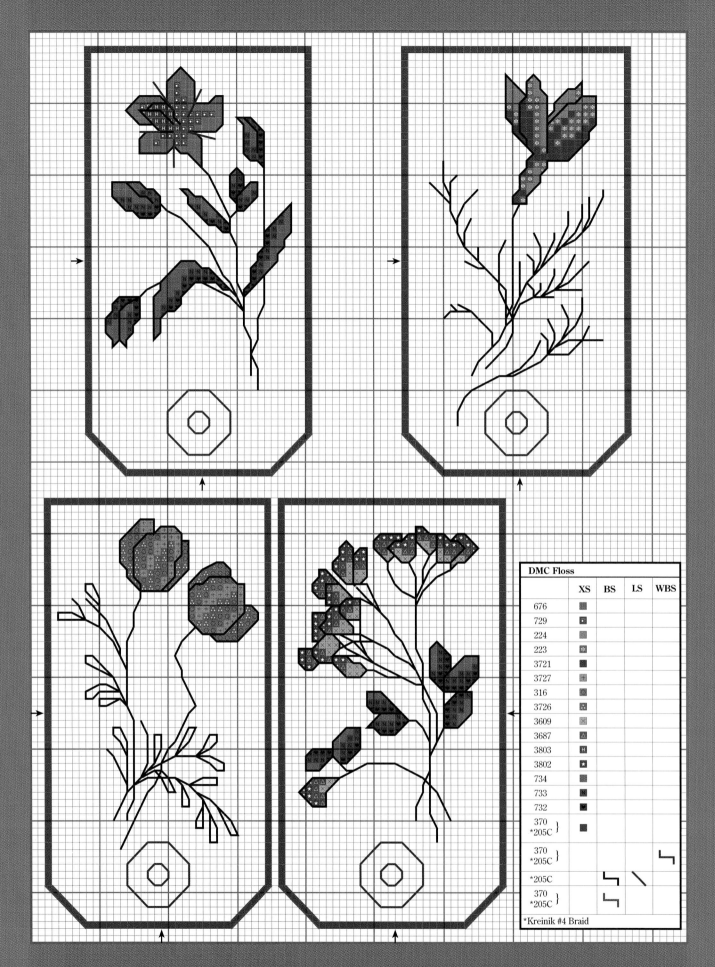

DMC Floss				
	XS	**BS**	**LS**	**WBS**
676	▓			
729	▣			
224	▨			
223	✳			
3721	▓			
3727	+			
316	◉			
3726	▨			
3609	⊠			
3687	▲			
3803	⊞			
3802	✦			
734	▓			
733	▓			
732	▣			
370 *205C }	▓			
370 *205C }				⌐
*205C		⌐	╱	
370 *205C }		⌐		
*Kreinik #4 Braid				

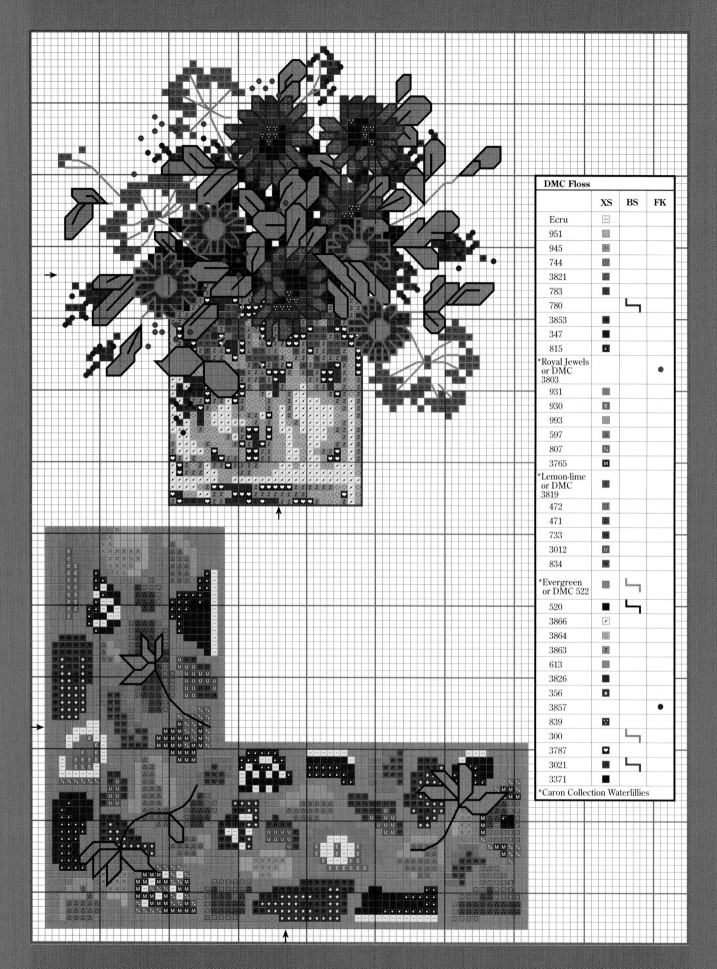

DMC Floss			
	XS	BS	FK
Ecru			
951			
945			
744			
3821			
783			
780			
3853			
347			
815			
*Royal Jewels or DMC 3803			
931			
930			
993			
597			
807			
3765			
*Lemon-lime or DMC 3819			
472			
471			
733			
3012			
834			
*Evergreen or DMC 522			
520			
3866			
3864			
3863			
613			
3826			
356			
3857			
839			
300			
3787			
3021			
3371			
*Caron Collection Waterlillies			

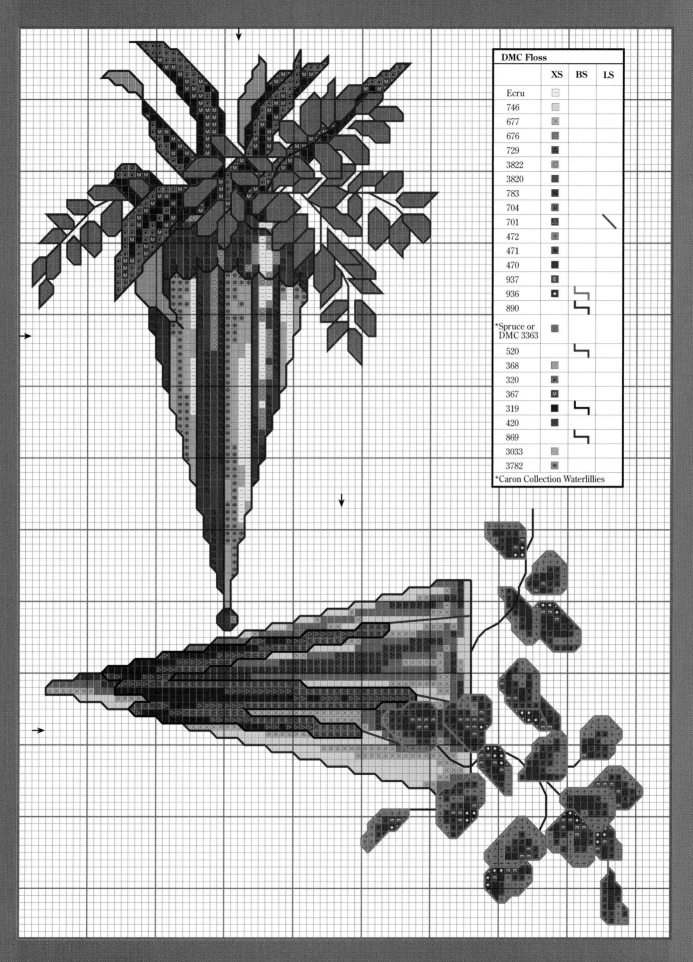

DMC Floss			
	XS	**BS**	**LS**
Ecru	⊟		
746	▦		
677	▨		
676	▦		
729	▨		
3822	◨		
3820	▦		
783	▦		
704	◨		
701	◭		╱
472	▨		
471	▨		
470	▦		
937	▣		
936	▩	⌐	
890		⌐	
*Spruce or DMC 3363	▦		
520		⌐	
368	▨		
320	▣		
367	M		
319	■	⌐	
420	▦		
869		⌐	
3033	▦		
3782	▨		
*Caron Collection Waterlillies			

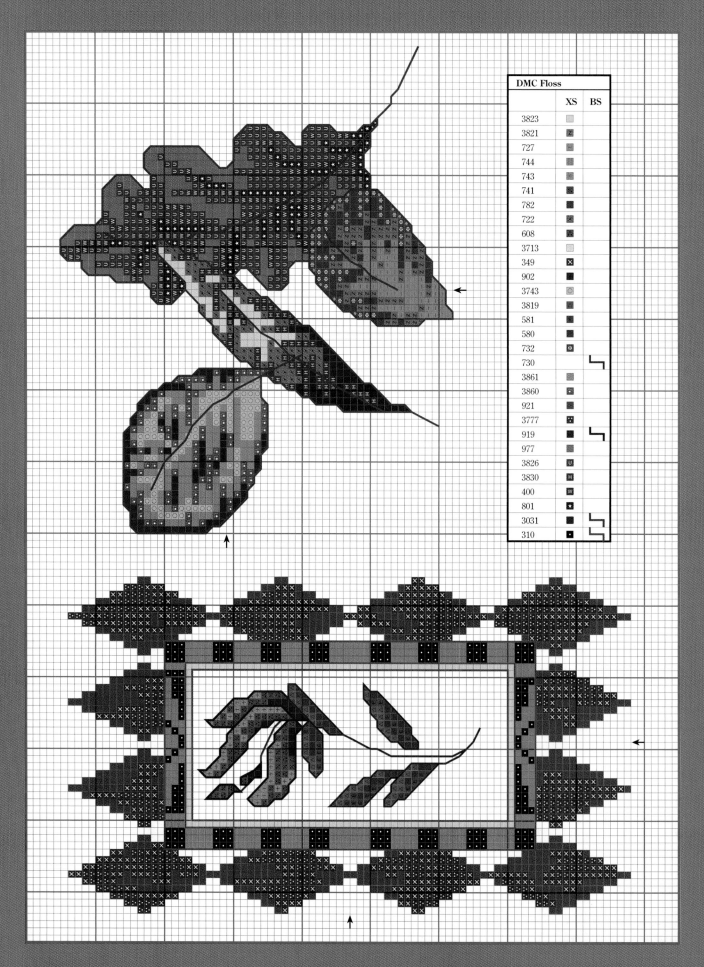

DMC Floss		
	XS	BS
3823		
3821	Z	
727		
744		
743		
741		
782		
722		
608		
3713		
349	X	
902		
3743	◎	
3819		
581		
580		
732		
730		⌐
3861		
3860		
921		
3777		
919		⌐
977		
3826	U	
3830	H	
400	W	
801		
3031		⌐
310		⌐

Caron Collection Waterlillies		
	XS	BS
Evergreen or DMC 368	▨	
*1844 or DMC 319		⌐
Succotash or DMC 471	▨	
*2125 or DMC 469		⌐
*Kreinik Silk		

Caron Collection Waterlillies			
	XS	BS	LS
Evergreen or DMC 368	▨		
*1844 or DMC 319		⌐	
Spruce or DMC 501		⌐	╲
*Kreinik Silk			

DMC Floss				
	XS	BS	FK	LS
White	·			
712				
745				
3821				
3820 } *002				
677				
676				
783				\
*002P				
3855			●	
3854				
3853				
900				
350	△			
817	H			
902		⌐		
341				
340				
598				
3849	N			
958	S			
939				
368		⌐		
936		⌐		
561				\
3819				
472				
471				
469				
3863				
3861		⌐		
422				
869		⌐		
918	★	⌐		
*Kreinik Blending Filament and Cable				

DMC Floss			DMC Floss			
	XS	BS		XS	BS	LS
White			3362			
712			976			
3822			3826			
729			739			
3855			738			
3854			437			
349			436			
734			433			
472			612			
3012			3860			
3011			839			
3364			645			
3363			310			

DMC Floss				DMC Floss			DMC Floss		
	XS	BS	FK		XS	BS		XS	BS
712				3348			500	E	
819			○	3347	H		3773		
353				3346			3772		
352				3345	*		433	N	
350				895	♥		632		
776				3012			838	W	
335				472			648		
304				471	M		646	△	
3685				934	★		844		
902									

DMC Floss				
	XS	BS	FK	LD
White	·			
3823				
745			◉	
677				
676				
729				
783				
772				
989	E			
503	△			
501	✳			
500		⌐		
3363				
3348	✕		◉	
3347				
3346		⌐		
3345	■	⌐		𝒪
924		⌐		
613				
612				
611	✕			
420	✦	⌐		
3021	■	⌐		

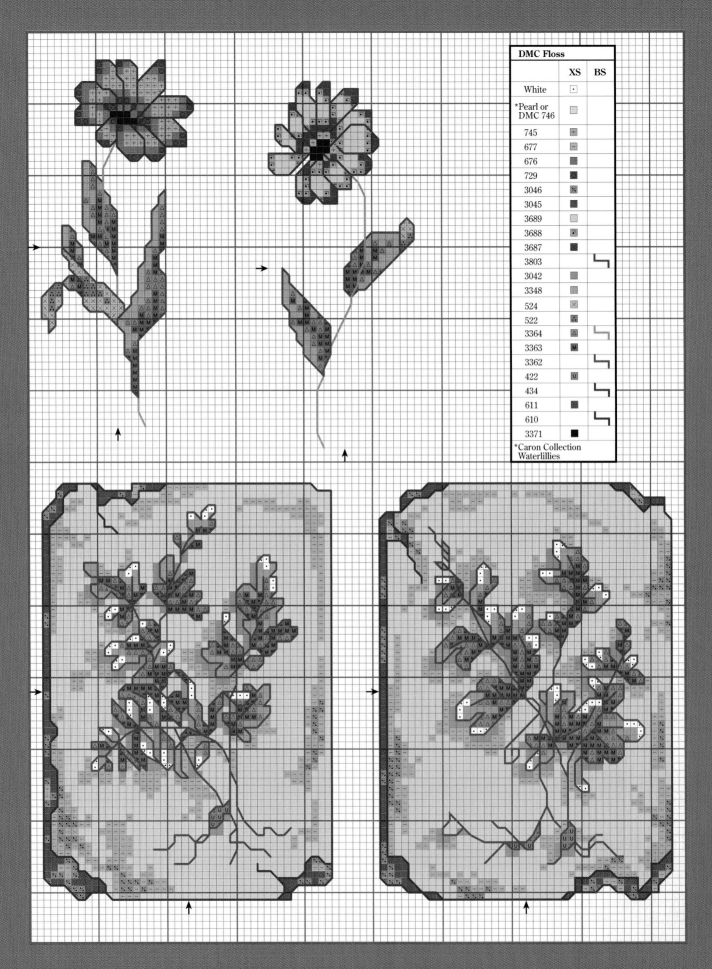

DMC Floss		
	XS	BS
White	·	
*Pearl or DMC 746		
745	+	
677		
676		
729		
3046		
3045		
3689		
3688	·	
3687		
3803		⌐
3042		
3348		
524	×	
522		
3364	△	⌐
3363	M	
3362		⌐
422	U	
434		⌐
611		
610		⌐
3371	■	⌐
*Caron Collection Waterlillies		

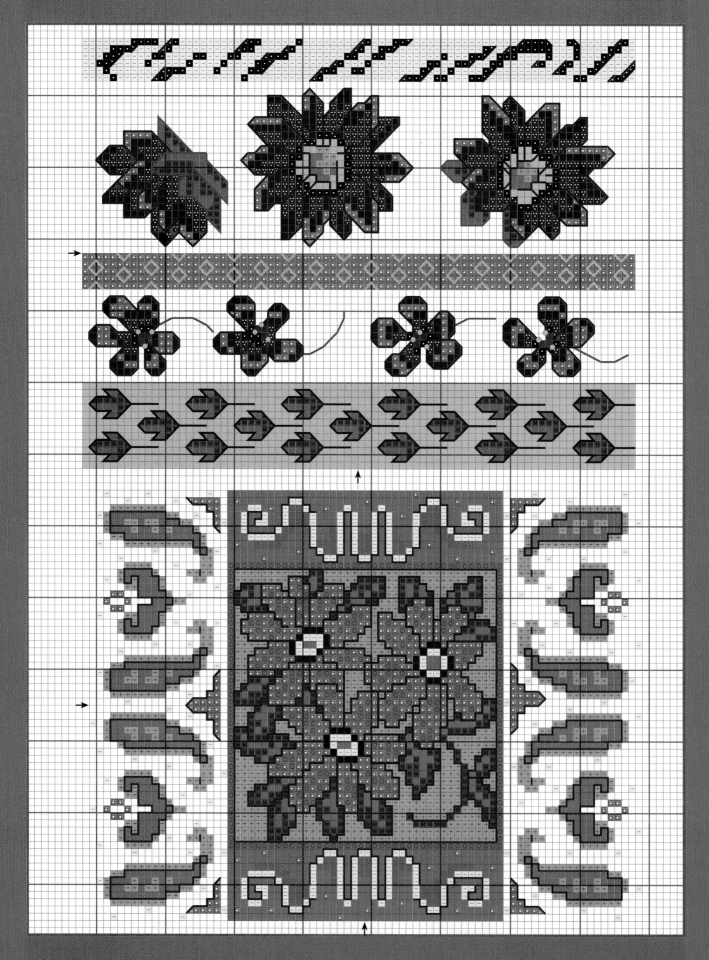

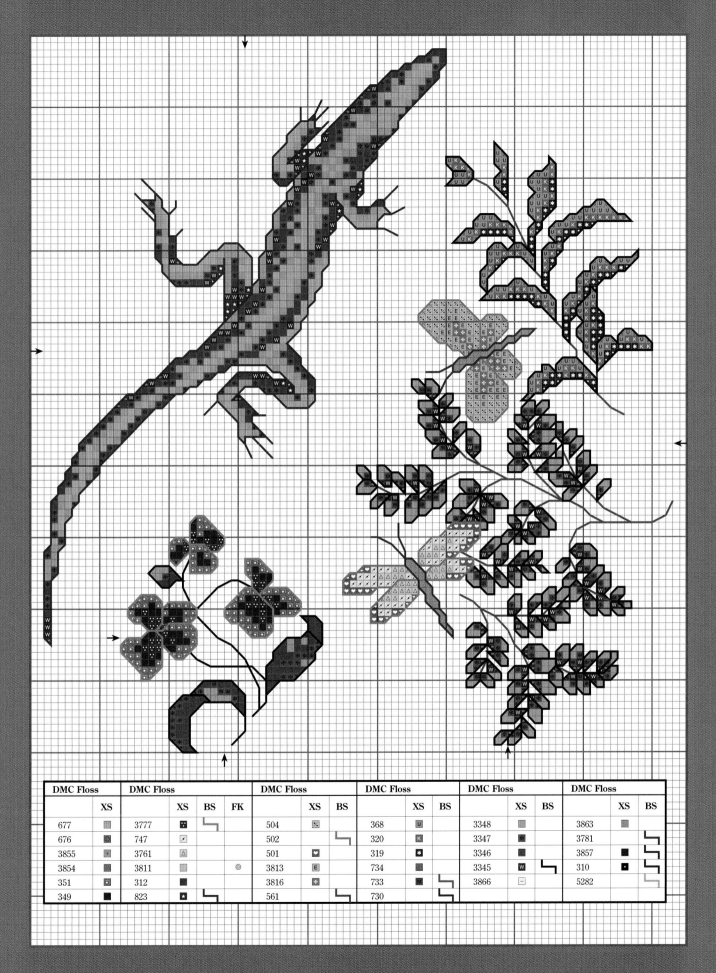

DMC Floss		DMC Floss				DMC Floss			DMC Floss			DMC Floss			DMC Floss		
	XS		XS	BS	FK		XS	BS		XS	BS		XS	BS		XS	BS
677		3777				504			368			3348			3863		
676		747				502			320			3347			3781		
3855		3761				501			319			3346			3857		
3854		3811				3813			734			3345			310		
351		312				3816			733			3866			5282		
349		823				561			730								

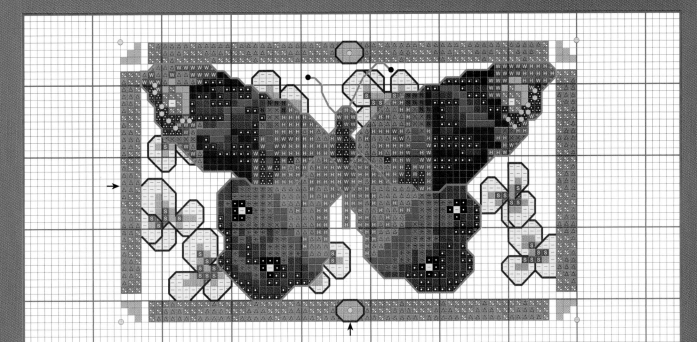

DMC Floss			
	XS	BS	FK
White	·		○
Ecru	⊟		●
745			
742			
725			
3852			
3853			
351			
350			
3831		⌐	
816			
902		⌐	●
519			
518			
3849		⌐	
3847		⌐	
834	S		
3776			
822			
610		⌐	
842			
841	M		
840	W		
839		⌐	
3072			
648			
647			
646	E		
645			
844		⌐	
310			●

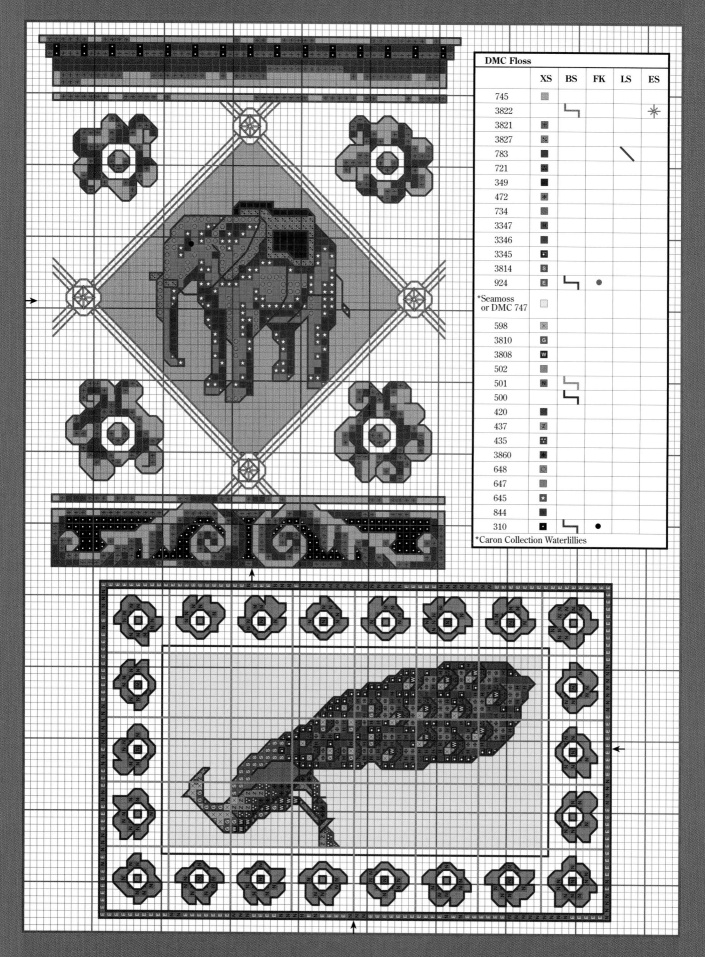

DMC Floss					
	XS	BS	FK	LS	ES
745	▦				
3822		⌐			✳
3821	▦				
3827	▦				
783	▦			╲	
721	▦				
349	▦				
472	✳				
734	▦				
3347	⋈				
3346	▦				
3345	▣				
3814	S				
924	E	⌐	●		
*Seamoss or DMC 747	▢				
598	⊠				
3810	G				
3808	W				
502	▦				
501	N	⌐			
500		⌐			
420	▦				
437	Z				
435	▣				
3860	▦				
648	◙				
647	▦				
645	★				
844	▦				
310	▪	⌐	●		
*Caron Collection Waterlillies					

American Landscape

DMC Floss			DMC Floss			DMC Floss			DMC Floss			DMC Floss		
	XS	FK		XS	BS		XS	BS		XS	BS		XS	BS
712	◪		3688	◉		340	E		472	▨		734	▲	
746		⊙	3687	▨		3740	▨		471	▨		733	▨	⌐
3078	⊞		3803	▣		793			470	H		732	M	
3823	▢		3802		⌐	792	★		937	W		3051		⌐
3822	▨		210	▨		3348	▨		936	▨		3829		⌐
3820	▨		208	▨		3347	▨		934		⌐	420		⌐
3689	▢		3747	⊞		3346	✦							

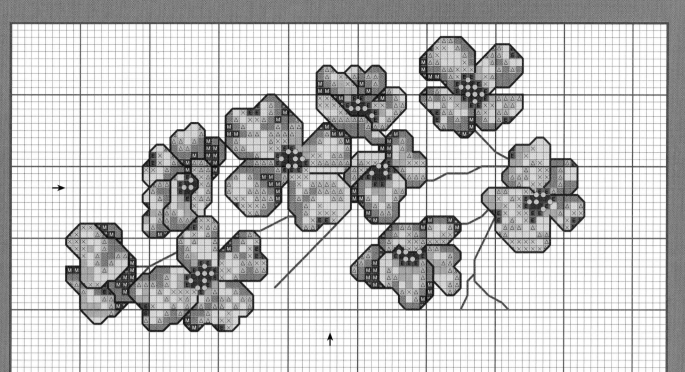

DMC Floss						DMC Floss			DMC Floss					DMC Floss			
	XS	BS	FK	SS			XS			XS	BS	FK			XS	BS
712	⊠		⊙	|||		818	▢		3687	▨				3813	▨	
3045						776	△		3803	M				704	E	
948	⊟					3326	N		814				●	*Succotash or DMC 471	▨	
353	⊞					899	▨		718							
352	◉					3354	▨		*Hyacinth or DMC 553	▨				937	▨	
3830	▨					3350	▨							3346	▨	
*Caron Collection Waterlillies																

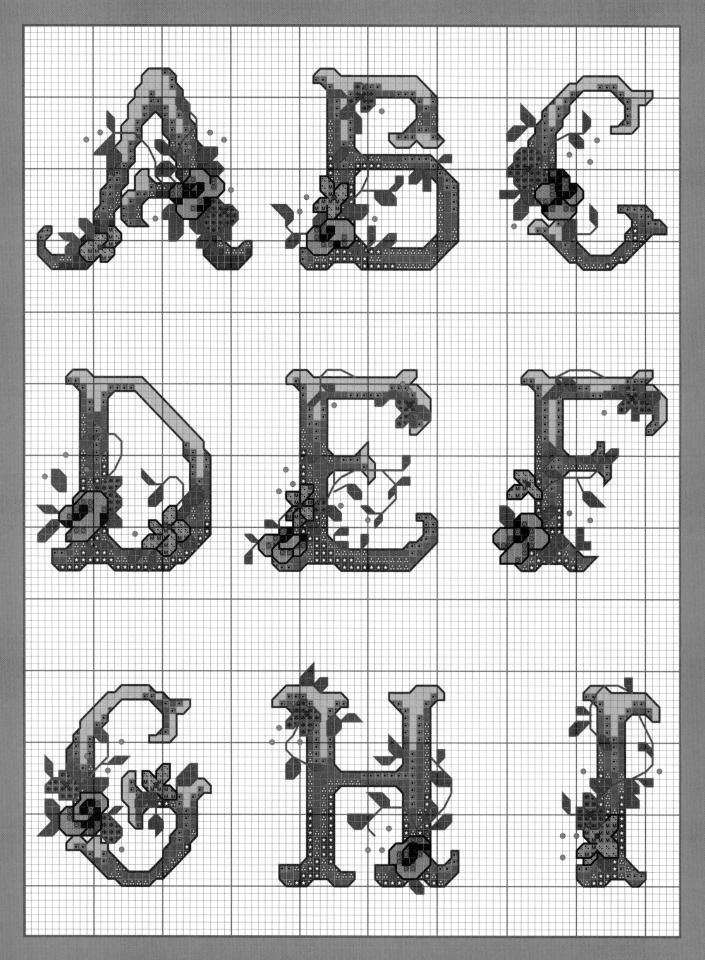

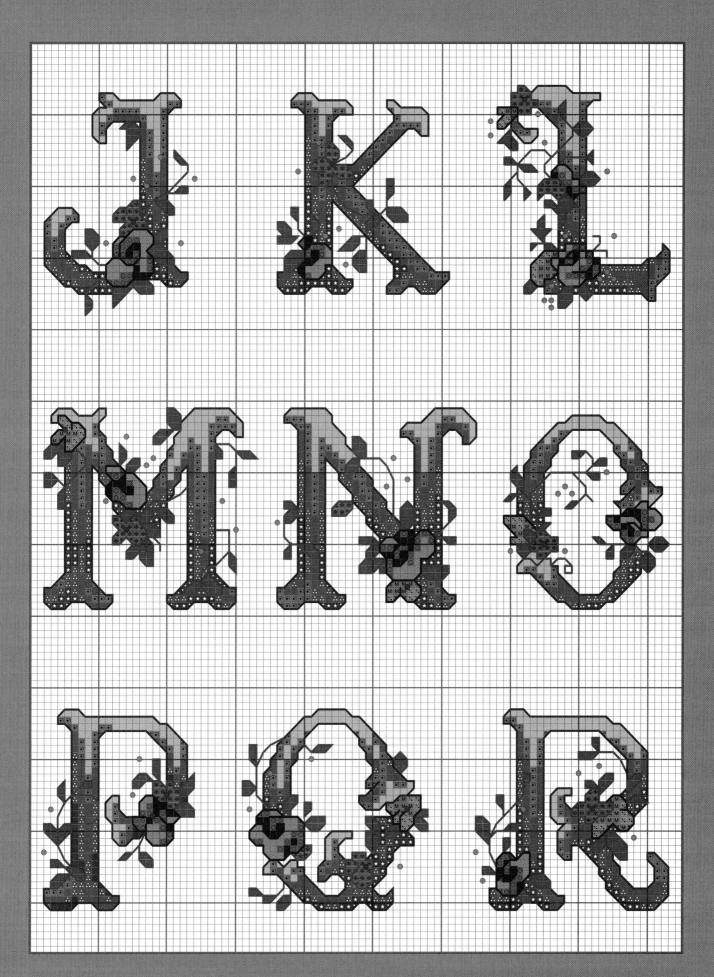

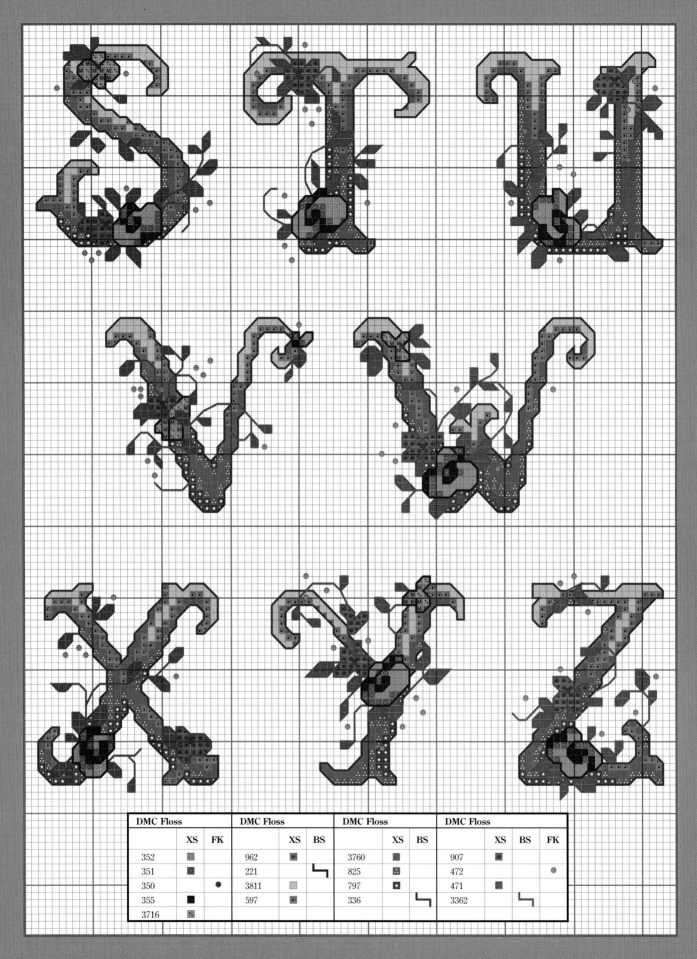

DMC Floss				DMC Floss				DMC Floss				DMC Floss			
	XS	FK			XS	BS			XS	BS			XS	BS	FK
352				962	M			3760				907			
351				221		⌐		825				472			●
350		●		3811				797				471			
355	■			597				336		⌐		3362		⌐	
3716															

48

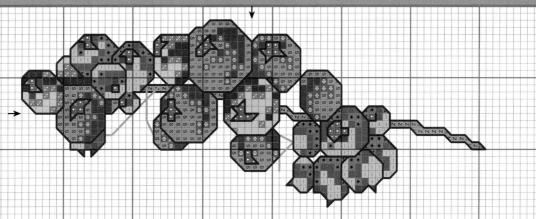

DMC Floss			DMC Floss			DMC Floss			DMC Floss			DMC Floss			
	XS	LS		XS	BS		XS	BS		XS	BS		XS	BS	FK
712			3041			794	S		926	H		772			
677			3740			3807			3819			3364	Z		
676			211			791			471			3363	★		
729			333			3811			734	M		3362			
3689			340			3813			371			3790	E		
316			747			*Spruce or DMC 3816			3051			869			●
*Caron Collection Waterlillies															

DMC Floss	XS	FK
712	⊟	◐
745		
743		
3046		●
948		
353		
352		

DMC Floss	XS
350	
3731	E
3350	■
3689	△
3688	
3687	

DMC Floss	XS	BS	FK	LS
3803				
902				
734				
834				
472			●	
471	S			

DMC Floss	XS	BS	LS
470			
469	■		
936			
3348			
3346	Z		
3345			

DMC Floss	XS	BS
739	U	
977	N	
976		
3778		
3777	M	
355	■	

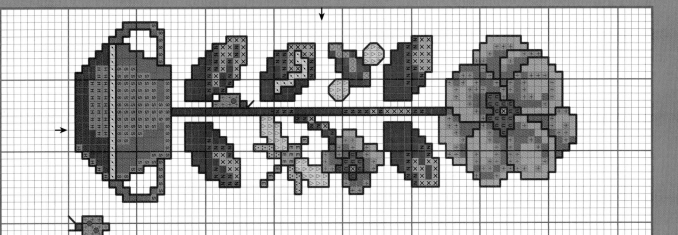

DMC Floss	XS	DMC Floss	XS	BS	DMC Floss	XS	BS	FK	DMC Floss	XS	BS	DMC Floss	XS	BS
*Pearl or DMC Ecru	—	352			210				794	Z		*Spruce or DMC 522		
712		351			3042	E			793			520		
*Lemon-lime or DMC745		818			3740			●	791			3827	S	
3822		3326			550				3819	U		977		
3820		335			3747				3348	X		422	H	
353		*Flame or DMC 326			340				3347	N		420		
		211			3746				367					

*Caron Collection Waterlillies

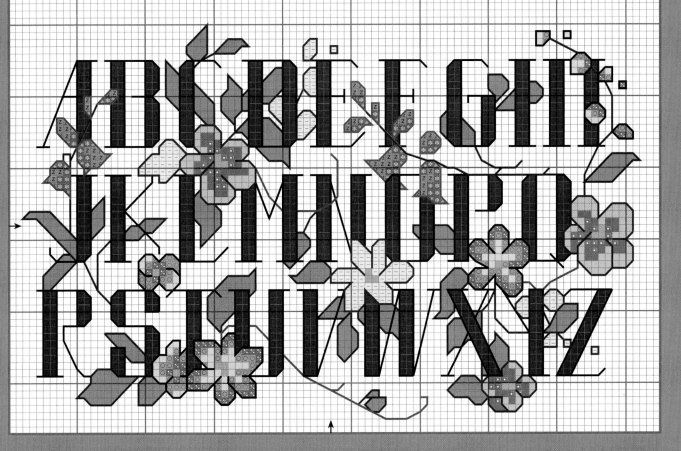

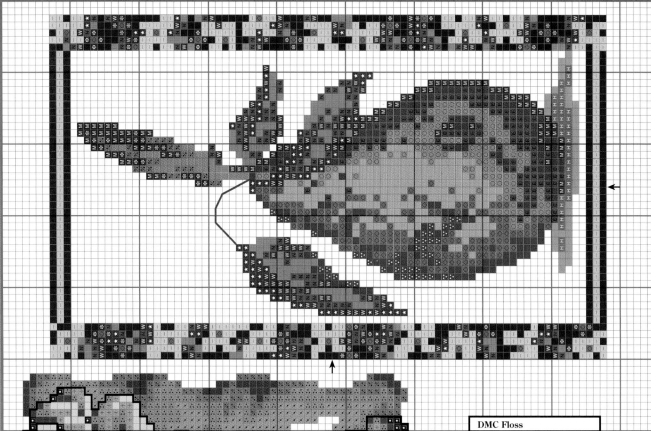

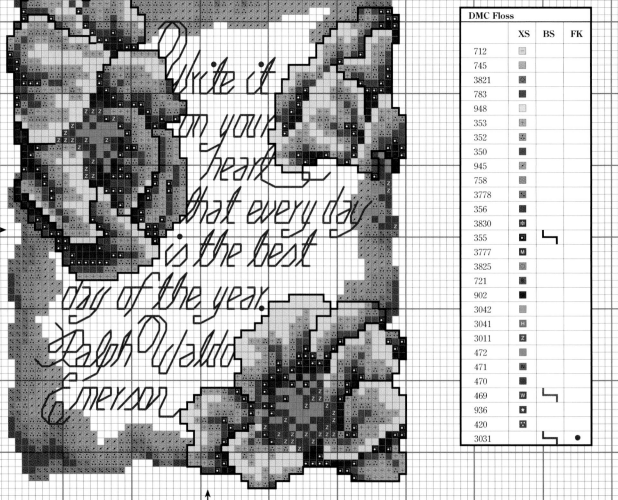

DMC Floss			
	XS	BS	FK
712			
745			
3821			
783			
948			
353			
352			
350			
945			
758			
3778			
356			
3830			
355		⌐	
3777	M		
3825			
721	E		
902			
3042			
3041	H		
3011	Z		
472			
471	N		
470			
469	W	⌐	
936			
420			
3031		⌐	●

DMC Floss			DMC Floss		
	XS	BS		XS	BS
White	·		926		
746			504		
445			503		
727			501	E	
726			734	K	
725	S		3051		⌐
3821			3347		
677			3345		
676	Z		472		
3829		⌐	471	B	
783			470		
781	N		937	M	
950			936	V	
3773			934	★	
225			833		
3727			830	W	
3726		⌐	739		
210			420		⌐
3041	U		301	A	
3740	✳		300	♥	
775			801		⌐
3325			3024		
794			3023		
3753	△		3022		
927	H		3787		

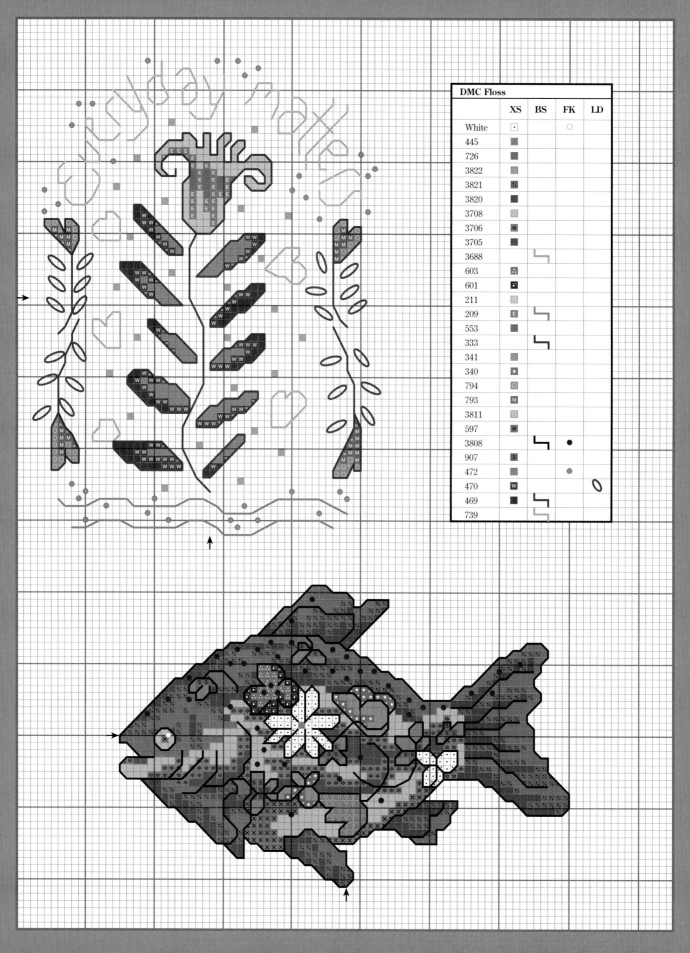

DMC Floss				
	XS	BS	FK	LD
White	⊡		○	
445				
726				
3822				
3821				
3820				
3708				
3706				
3705				
3688		⌐		
603				
601				
211				
209	E	⌐		
553				
333		⌐		
341				
340				
794	◉			
793	M			
3811				
597	✕			
3808		⌐	●	
907	S			
472			●	
470	W			⬭
469		⌐		
739		⌐		

DMC Floss					
	XS	BS	FK	LS	SS
White	·		○		‖‖‖
746					
445					
3823	✕				
3821				╱	
3047	◙				
3046					
371		⌐			
472					
471	✕				
470					
469	★				
937		⌐			
3053	△				
3052	·				
3051	M				
934	♥				

DMC Floss			
	XS	**BS**	**FK**
White	·		○
*Mode or DMC Ecru	⊟		
*2242 or DMC 2242	▦		
350	▦		
355	✿		
3706	▨		
3722	▨		
818	▨		
776	⊞		
*2941 or DMC 776	◭		
*2943 or DMC 899	▨		
*2944 or DMC 335	✳		
*2945 or DMC 309	Z		
*2925 or DMC 3803	▣	⌐	
*4631 or DMC 778	◉		
*4633 or DMC 316	▨		
902	■	⌐	
*1432 or DMC 3752	▨		
*1433 or DMC 931	M		
*1715 or DMC 3750		⌐	
*1441 or DMC 928	▨		
*1744 or DMC 927	S		
*1745 or DMC 3768	▨		
*1746 or DMC 924	▨	⌐	
*1842 or DMC 3813	▨		
*1843 or DMC 502	U		
*1844 or DMC 501	W	⌐	
*1841 or DMC 369	◈		
*2212 or DMC 734	E		
*2225 or DMC 831		⌐	
3348	▦		
3347	▦		
3346	✿		
3345	■	⌐	
*4114 or DMC 840	▨	⌐	
*Kreinik Silk			

DMC Floss		
	XS	BS
White	·	
727		
3820		
781		⌐
758		
353		
352		
351		
350		
349		
817	M	
963		
3706		
3705	H	
3726		
3802		⌐
902		⌐
3348	△	
3011	N	
472		
471		
470		⌐
469		
936	W	⌐
3364	U	
3363		⌐
3362		⌐

DMC Floss			DMC Floss			DMC Floss		
	XS	BS		XS	BS		XS	BS
White	·		211			501		
746			210			472		
745	H		3042	E		470	S	
743			3041		⌐	937	H	
742			3761			936	♥	⌐
677			3755			935		
676			322			921		
3689			311	★	⌐	919	N	
3688	✳		793	U		422		
3687			792			3828	✚	
3803	M		791	W	⌐	420		
3685		⌐	369			3781		⌐
902		⌐	368					

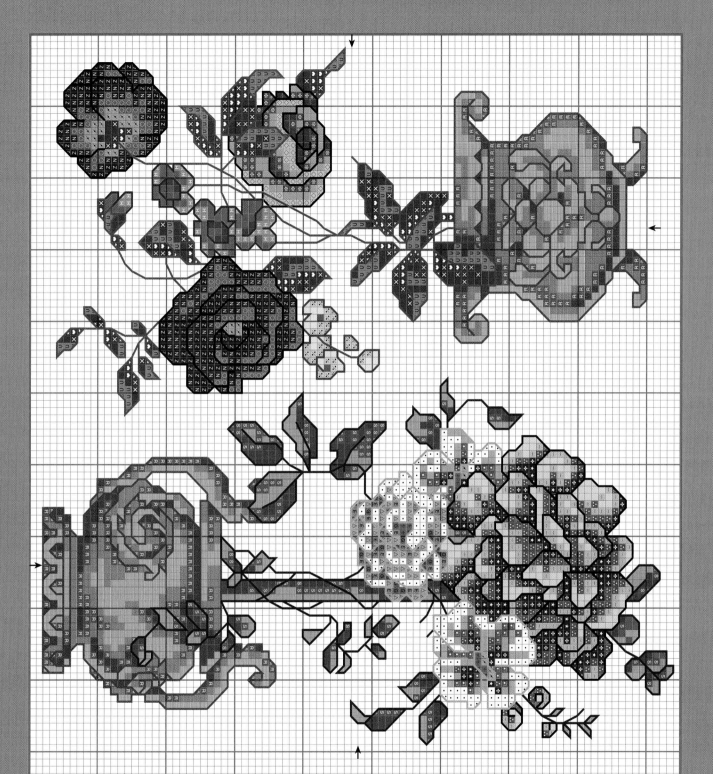

DMC Floss		DMC Floss		DMC Floss			DMC Floss			DMC Floss			DMC Floss		
	XS		XS		XS	BS		XS	BS		XS	BS		XS	BS
White	·	818		3687			794	H		3053			407	G	
745		3708		3803			793			520			422		
3821		3705		221	Z		791			472	U		3828	R	
725		351		902			931			470			420		
677		349	N	747			3348			469	X		3781		
783		347		3761			3347	S		936	♥		632		
3824	△	3689	◇	3755			3346			935			3024		
3341	E	3688													

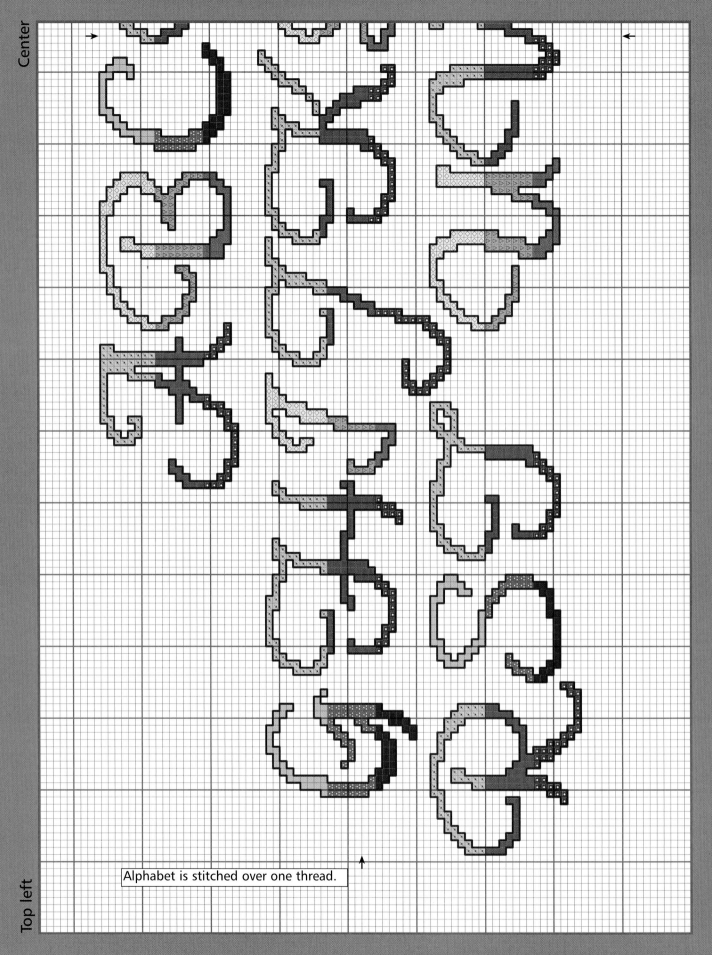

Alphabet is stitched over one thread.

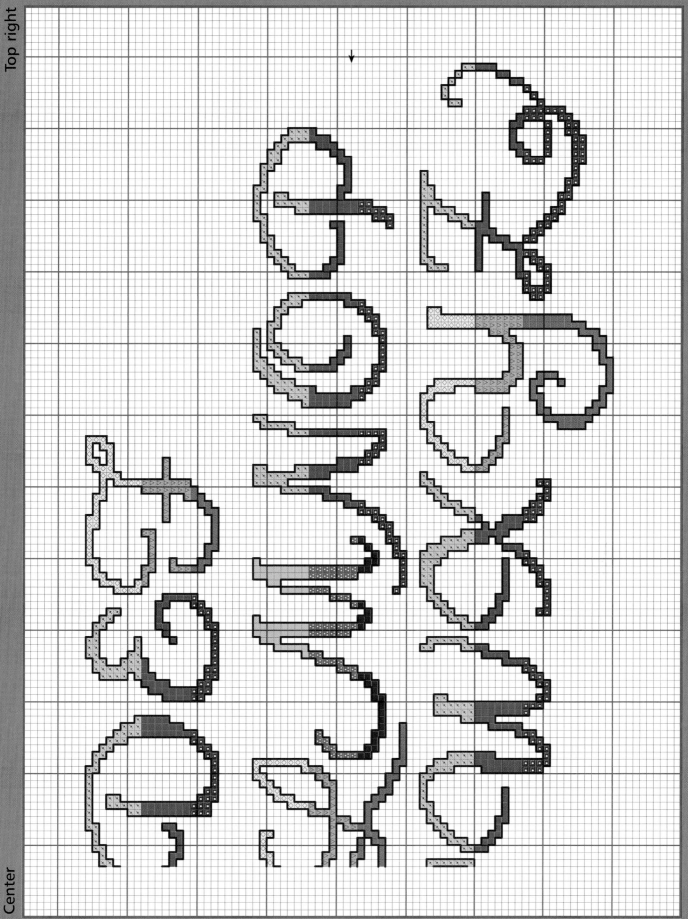

DMC Floss	XS	TS (Over 1 Thread)	BS	FK
Ecru	–	◇		
3823	▣			
3822	✳			
3820	■			●
352	▨			
351	▨			
321	■			●
321 } 814	✛			
814			⌐	
778	⬚	V		
316	S	▨		
211	+	▨		○
209 } 553	◉	▨		
333	★	■	⌐	
3042	U			
3041	W			
3740			⌐	
3747	✕	✕		○
793	△	▨		
792	M	▣		
931 } 501	Z			
930	♥		⌐	
3348	▨			
368	▨			
320	▨		⌐	
501	N		⌐	
738	J			
436	E			
3041 } 436	✛			
822	▨			
3782	▨			
3032 } 640	H			
3787			⌐	

DMC Floss	XS	TS (Over 1 Thread)	BS	FK
Ecru	–	◇		
3823				
3822				
3820				●
352				
351				
321				●
321 814 }				
814			⌐	
778		V		
316	S			
211	+			○
209 553 }	○			
333	★		⌐	
3042	U			
3041	W			
3740			⌐	
3747	✕			○
793	▲			
792	M			
931 501 }	Z			
930	♥		⌐	
3348				
368				
320			⌐	
501	N			
738	J			
436	E			
3041 436 }				
822				
3782				
3032 640 }	H			
3787			⌐	

Each Flower is a soc

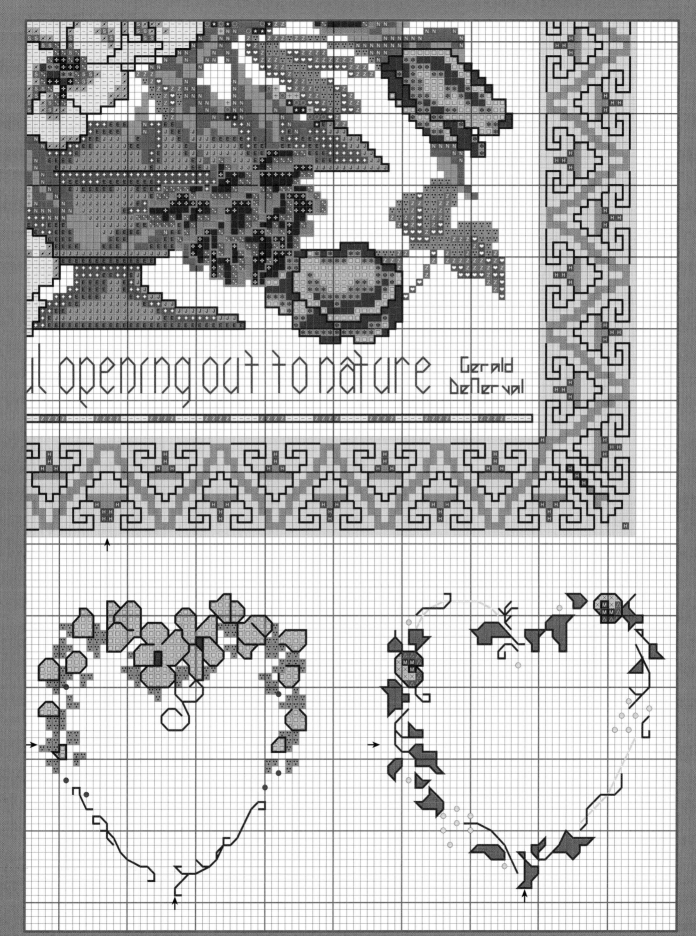

...l opening out to nature — Gerald DeNerval

Bottom right

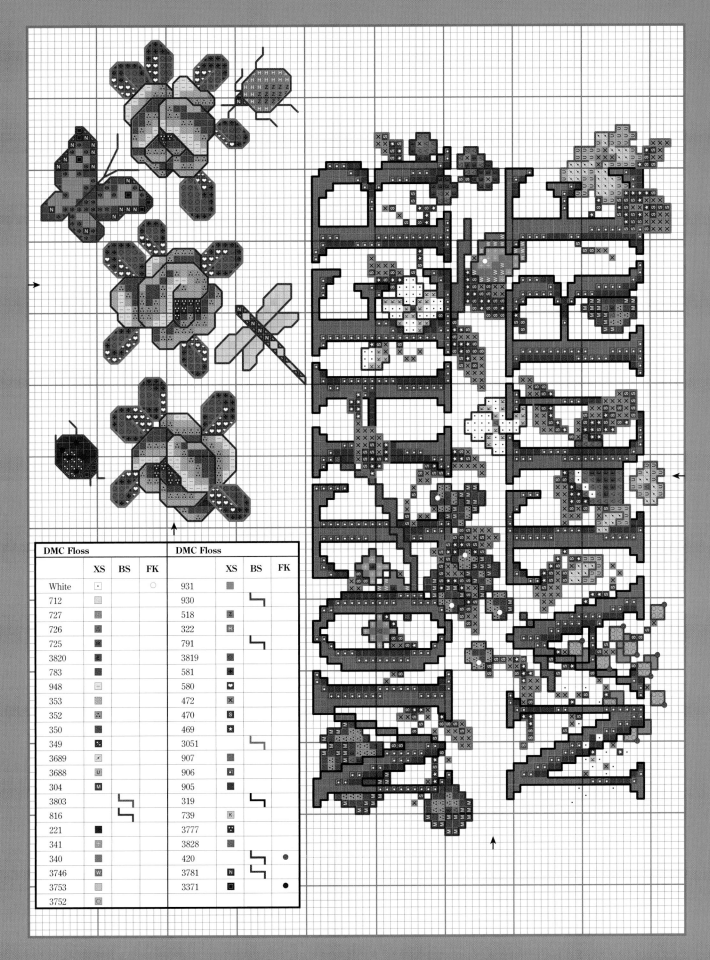

DMC Floss				DMC Floss			
	XS	**BS**	**FK**		**XS**	**BS**	**FK**
White	·		○	931			
712				930		⌐	
727				518	Z		
726	A			322	H		
725				791		⌐	
3820	E			3819			
783				581			
948	–			580	♥		
353				472	X		
352				470	S		
350				469	★		
349				3051			
3689				907			
3688	U			906			
304	M			905			
3803		⌐		319		⌐	
816		⌐		739	K		
221				3777			
341	+			3828			
340				420		⌐	●
3746	W			3781	N		
3753				3371		⌐	●
3752	O						

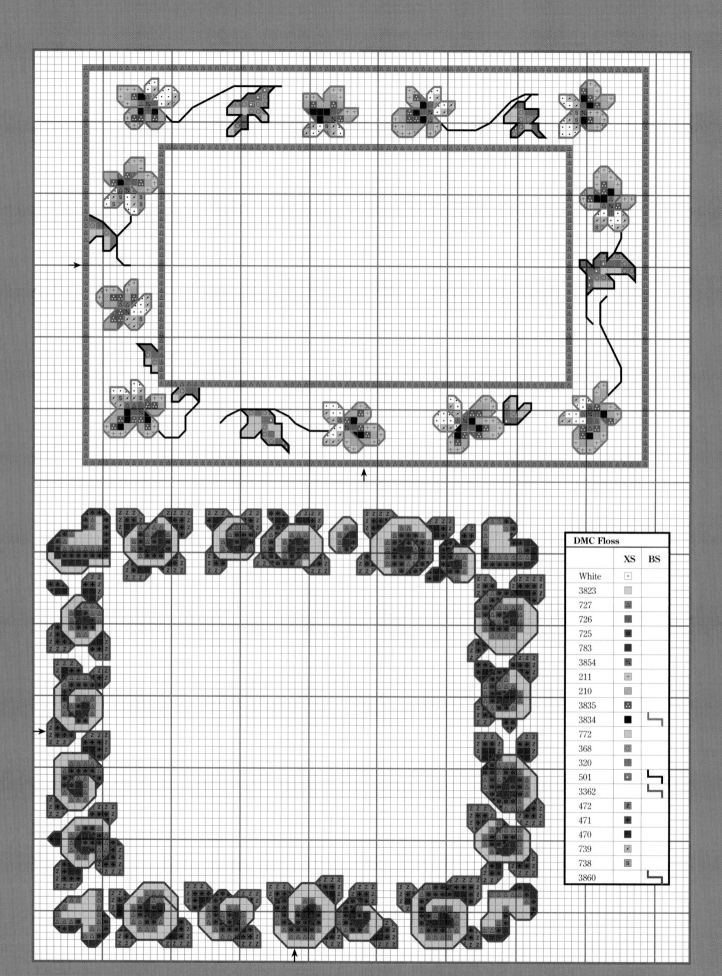

DMC Floss		
	XS	BS
White	·	
3823		
727		
726		
725		
783		
3854		
211	+	
210		
3835		
3834	■	
772		
368		
320		
501		
3362		
472	z	
471		
470	■	
739		
738	S	
3860		

DMC Floss				
	XS	BS	FK	LS
White	·			
677				
727				
726				
951				
945				
3773				
3854				
3853				
351				
349				
815	·			
902		⌐		
211	U			
210				
3835				
3834		⌐		
772	◇			
3348	S			
368				
320		⌐		╱
501		⌐		
500		⌐		
739	X			
738	E			
3860		⌐	●	

DMC Floss					DMC Floss		
	XS	BS	FK			XS	BS
White	·				3746	▫	
Ecru	⊟				791	★	⌐
725	▦				3348	▨	
676	▨				3347	▦	
783	▦				3346	▦	
760	▨				472	U	
352	▦				471	▦	
351	▦				470	M	
3328	▨				368	◩	
3830	▦				501	⊞	⌐
3803	▦	⌐			500		⌐
814		⌐	●		435	E	
3042	▲				869	S	⌐
3747	▫				310	▪	⌐
340	▦						

72

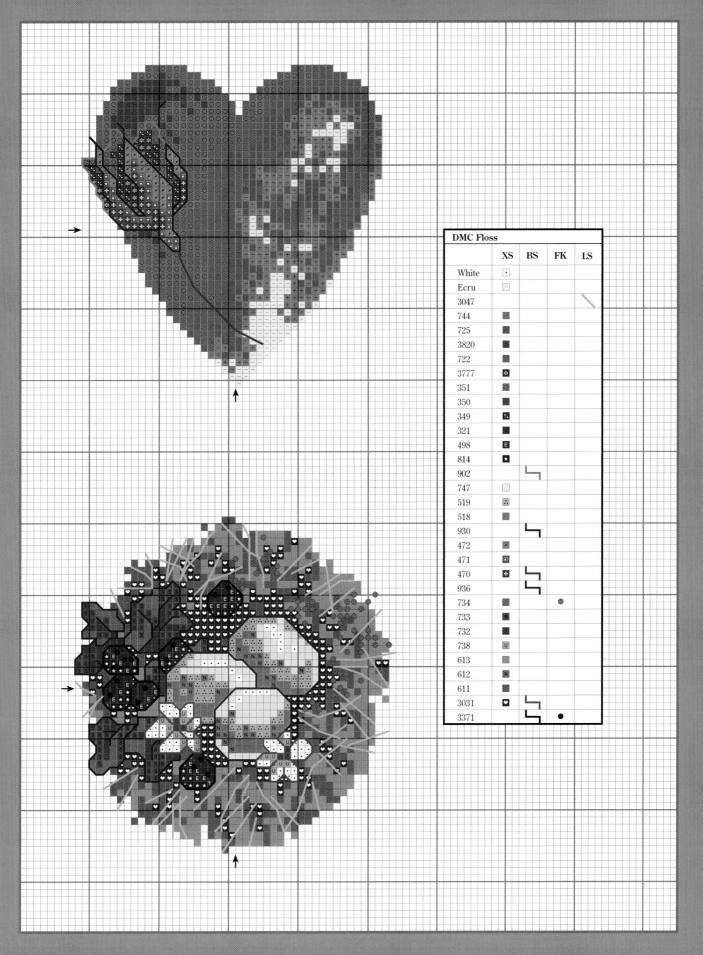

DMC Floss	XS	BS	FK	LS
White	·			
Ecru	⊟			
3047				╲
744	▦			
725	▦			
3820	▦			
722	▦			
3777	✹			
351	◩			
350	▦			
349	▨			
321	◼			
498	E			
814	★			
902		⌐		
747	▢			
519	⊡			
518	▦			
930		⌐		
472	◪			
471	◲			
470	✸	⌐		
936		⌐		
734	▦		●	
733	◐			
732	▦			
738	U			
613	▦			
612	N			
611	▦			
3031	♥	⌐		
3371		⌐	●	

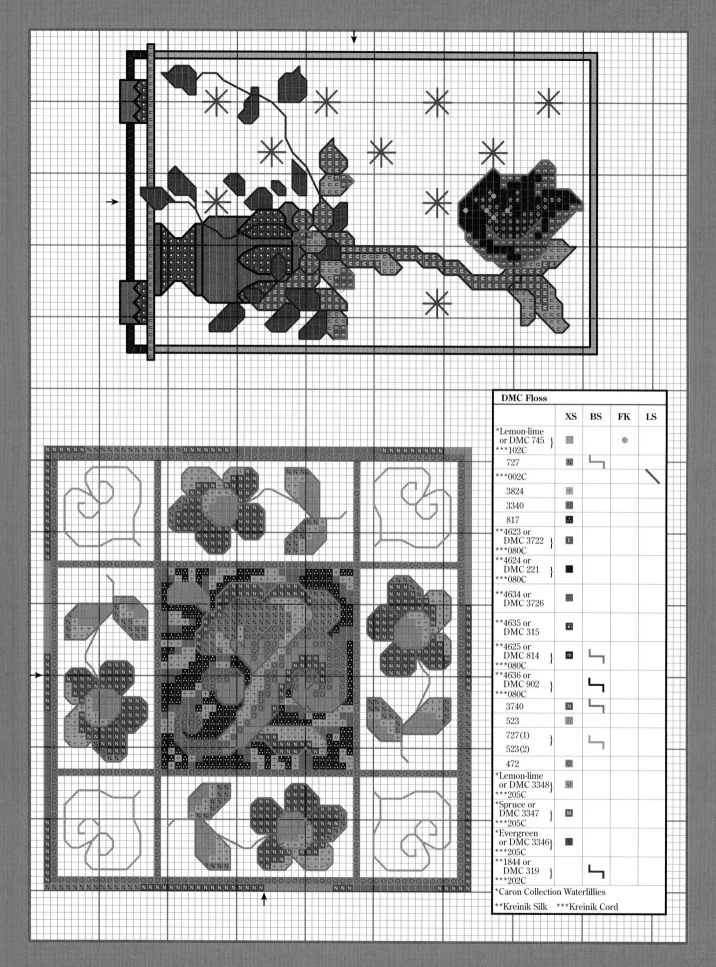

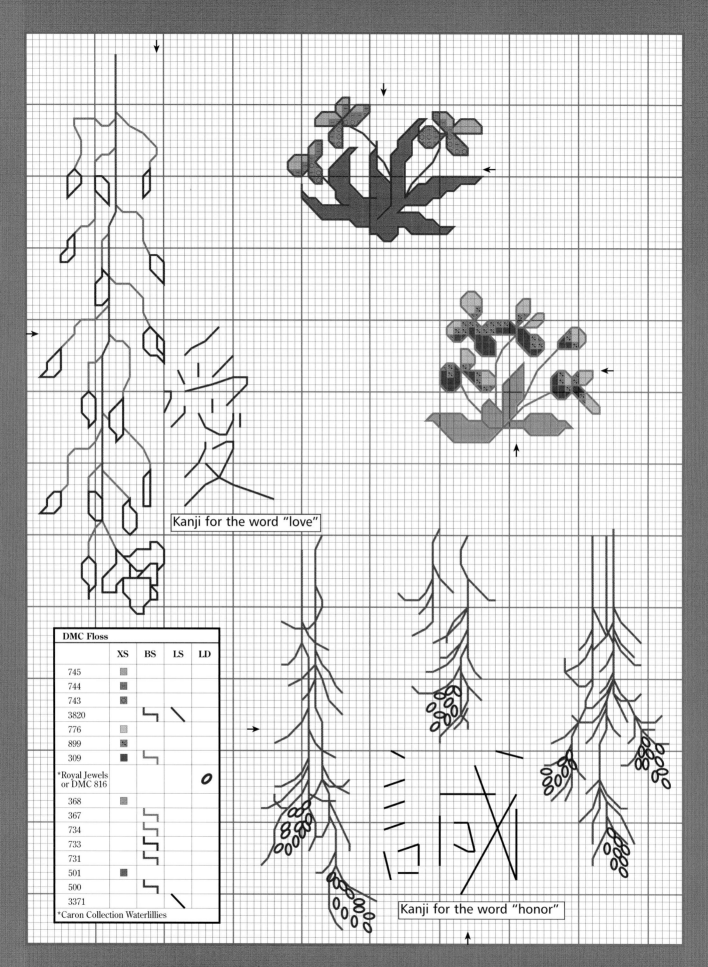

Kanji for the word "love"

Kanji for the word "honor"

DMC Floss				
	XS	BS	LS	LD
745	▥			
744	▤			
743	◙			
3820		⌐	╲	
776	▨			
899	▦			
309	▩	⌐		
*Royal Jewels or DMC 816				𝑂
368	▦			
367		⌐		
734		⌐		
733		⌐		
731		⌐		
501	▦			
500		⌐		
3371			╲	
*Caron Collection Waterlillies				

76

DMC Floss	
	XS
White	·
3770	
744	
3825	
721	
720	
819	▬
604	
3689	
3687	
315	✳
3042	
3819	
581	
733	E
472	
471	H
833	
3011	★
*Spruce or DMC 368	
3363	S
3362	
822	
3830	
3777	△
3022	
3787	■
*Caron Collection Waterlillies	

DMC Floss				
	XS	BS	FK	LS
White	·			
712	+			
3078				
3822				
3821				
3820				
606			●	
472				
734				
832				
3011		⌐		
772				
955	⊙			
3348				
3347	m			
3346				
3345				
895				
369	Z			
368				/
320	H	⌐		/
319				
503	⚠			
500		⌐		

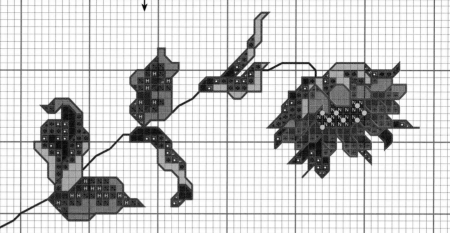

Trust in your heart.

DMC Floss	XS	BS	FK	LS	DMC Floss	XS	BS	FK	DMC Floss	XS	BS	DMC Floss	XS	BS	LS
White	·			/	924		⌐	●	320	▦		613	▦		
712			●		472	▦			367	▣		612	Z		
727	▦				733	▨			319	M	⌐	611	✦		
725	▦				831	H			500		⌐	610	▦		
783	▦		●		3347	▨	⌐		822	▢		433	N		
3045		⌐			890	■	⌐		644	△		413	▦		
780		⌐			3817	▢			642	E		310	■	⌐	/
312	▦				368	▦									

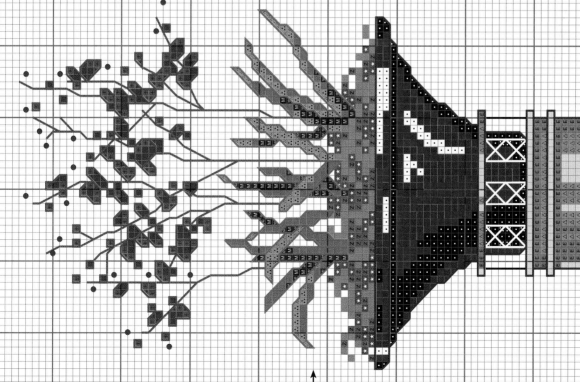

DMC Floss			DMC Floss			DMC Floss			DMC Floss			
	XS	FK		XS	BS		XS	BS		XS	BS	FK
White	·		3721	▣		3042	S		734	Z		
445	▣	●	221		⌐	3041	▣		832	▣		
760	◎		3688	+		3740		⌐	3347	✳	⌐	
3328	✳		3687	▣		*Succotash or DMC 471	▣		3051		⌐	
*Sandstone or DMC 225	▣		3803	N	⌐				3362		⌐	
			211	▢		472	▨		520		⌐	●
*Far Horizons or DMC 899	▣		210	△		471	▣		611	▣		
*Caron Collection Waterlillies												

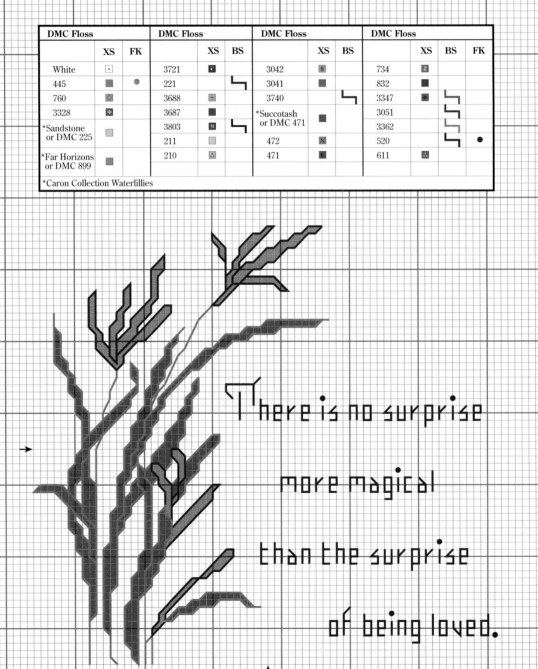

There is no surprise

more magical

than the surprise

of being loved.

DMC Floss				
	XS	**BS**	**FK**	**LS**
Ecru	⊡		○	
3078	▥			
745	◪			
744	▨			
3046	⊞			
*Prairie Fire or DMC 922	▨			
817	U			
962	◉			
3350	▧			
3803	E			
3685		⌐		
221	■	⌐	●	
793	▨			
791		⌐		
772	▨			
369	◹			
*Spruce or DMC 320	▨			
524	⊡			
522	N	⌐		
*Evergreen or DMC 502	▨			
3362		⌐		
472	▨			
471		⌐		
936	▪			
3348	◈			
3347	▨			
3346	✦			
3345	▨			
895		⌐		
831			●	
437	H			
436		⌐		
435	▨			
**022BF				╲
644	K			
640	▨			
898		⌐		
453	▦			
647	⊞			
3787	■			
310	▪	⌐		
*Caron Collection Waterlillies				
**Kreinik Blending Filament				

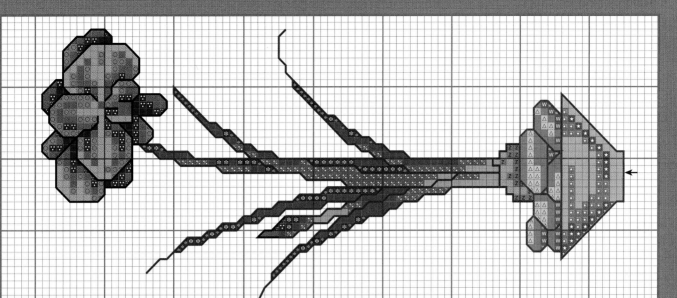

DMC Floss			DMC Floss			DMC Floss			DMC Floss		
	XS	BS		XS	BS		XS	BS		XS	BS
353			3813			3347			436		
899			926			3346			3072		
335			3768			3345			647		
326			924			895			645		
814			3348			738			844		

Kreinik Silk			
	XS	**BS**	**FK**
Blanc or DMC White	·		
Creme or DMC Ecru	–		
4635 or DMC 315		⌐	
4911 or DMC 3840	▣		
4912 or DMC 3839	▣		
4921 or DMC 800	△		
4922 or DMC 799	▣		
4923 or DMC 798	N	⌐	
1423 or DMC 312	★		
1714 or DMC 931	❄		
1715 or DMC 930		⌐	
1425 or DMC 823	W	⌐	●
F10 or DMC 739	▦		
4642 or DMC 543	◎		
2611 or DMC 3827	✜		
2612 or DMC 977	▣		
4115 or DMC 839		⌐	

There is a silence,

born of love,

which expresses

everything.

DMC Floss			DMC Floss			DMC Floss			DMC Floss		
	XS	FK		XS	BS		XS	BS		XS	BS
White	·	○	471	▓		3051		⌐	520	■	
Ecru	–		470	▓		772	▒		834	M	
3770	▒		937		⌐	524	+		830		⌐
3819	▓		936		⌐	523	△		730		
581	▓		3053		⌐	522	✳		3024	▒	
472	▓										

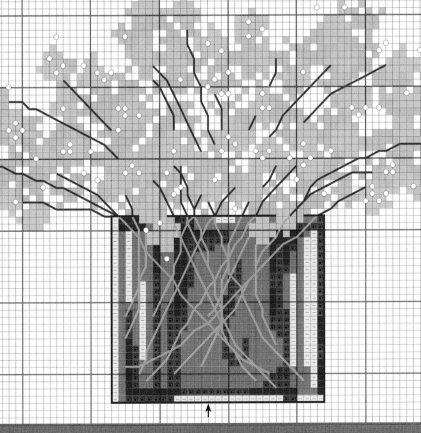

DMC Floss				
	XS	**BS**	**FK**	**SS**
White	·			
Ecru			○	
3820				
680				
819				
3609				
3608				
718				
915				
*Tobacco or DMC 3836				
554				
553	Z			
552	✳			
550	♥			
598				
597				
3810				
3809	M			
472				
470	S			
*Caron Collection Waterlillies				

DMC Floss

	XS	BS	FK
712			⊙
225			
224			
223			
3722	E		
3721	★		
221		⌐	
554			
553	△		
552			
550	■	⌐	
*Java or DMC 522		⌐	
739			
543	◎		
842			
841			

*Caron Collection Waterlillies

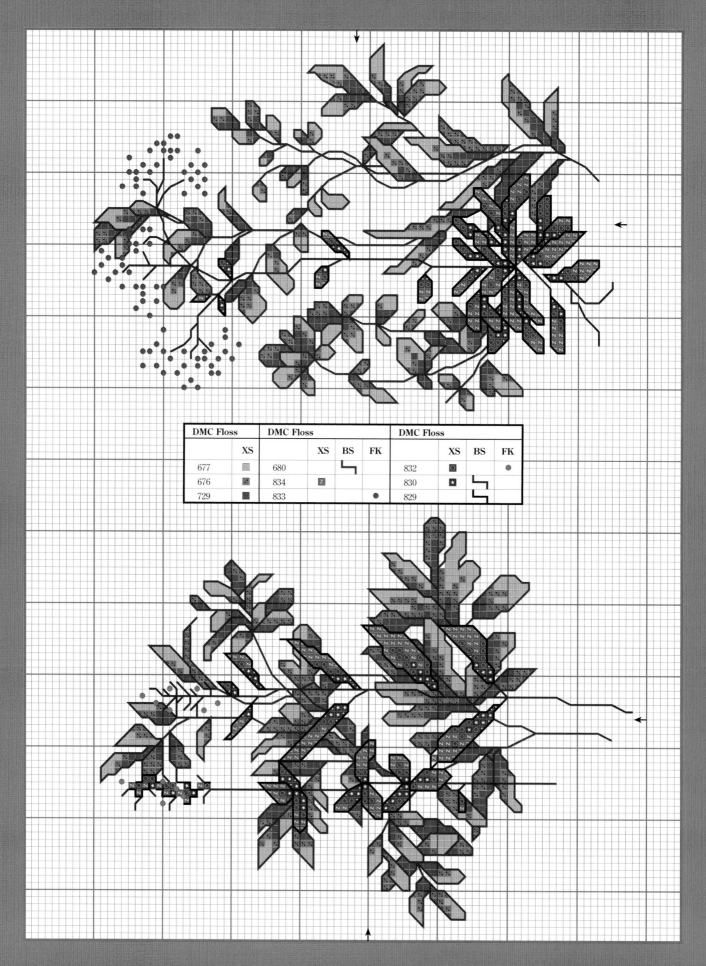

DMC Floss		DMC Floss				DMC Floss			
	XS		XS	BS	FK		XS	BS	FK
677		680		⌐		832	◙		●
676		834	Z			830	★	⌐	
729		833			●	829			

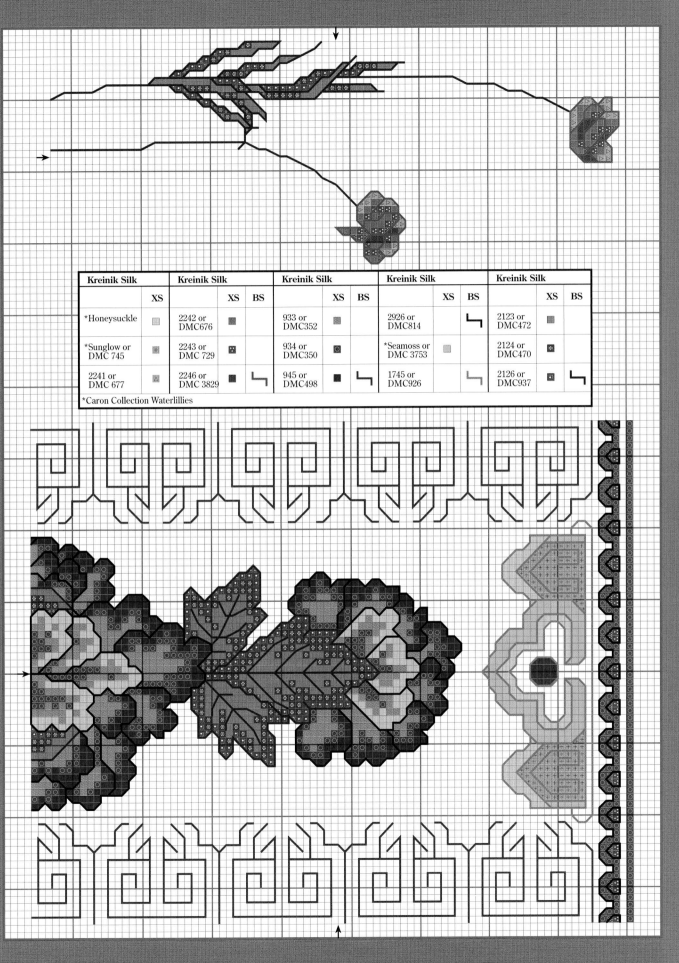

Kreinik Silk			Kreinik Silk			Kreinik Silk			Kreinik Silk			Kreinik Silk		
	XS			XS	BS		XS	BS		XS	BS		XS	BS
*Honeysuckle			2242 or DMC676			933 or DMC352			2926 or DMC814			2123 or DMC472		
*Sunglow or DMC 745			2243 or DMC 729			934 or DMC350			*Seamoss or DMC 3753			2124 or DMC470		
2241 or DMC 677			2246 or DMC 3829			945 or DMC498			1745 or DMC926			2126 or DMC937		

*Caron Collection Waterlillies

89

Kreinik Silk			
	XS	**BS**	**FK**
Mode or DMC 712	▨	⌐	
*Sunglow or DMC 745	⊞		
4232 or DMC 3822	◉		
3816 or DMC 434		⌐	●
*Pistachio Nut or DMC 341	▨		
1234 or DMC 437	⊠		
4523 or DMC 3863	▨		
3434 or DMC 840	✳		
3436 or DMC 838	■		
4136 or DMC 3371	✶	⌐	
4115 or DMC 3031		⌐	
*Caron Collection Waterlillies			

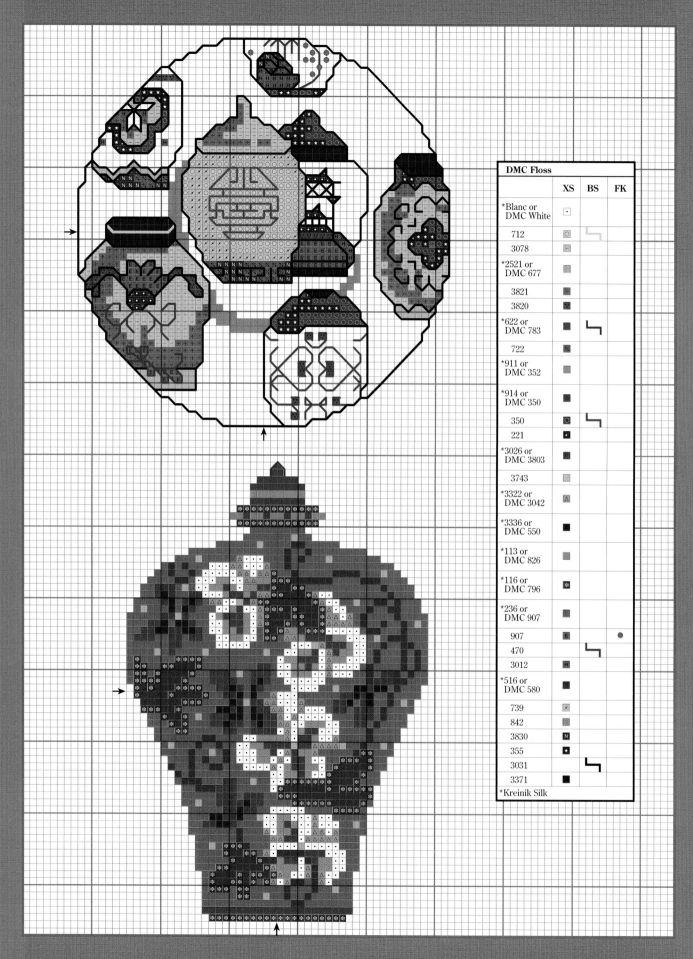

DMC Floss			
	XS	BS	FK
*Blanc or DMC White	⊡		
712	◎		
3078	⊞		
*2521 or DMC 677			
3821			
3820			
*622 or DMC 783		⌐	
722			
*911 or DMC 352			
*914 or DMC 350			
350	◎	⌐	
221			
*3026 or DMC 3803			
3743			
*3322 or DMC 3042	◺		
*3336 or DMC 550			
*113 or DMC 826			
*116 or DMC 796	✳		
*236 or DMC 907			
907	E		●
470		⌐	
3012	H		
*516 or DMC 580			
739	◪		
842			
3830	N		
355	★		
3031		⌐	
3371	■		
*Kreinik Silk			

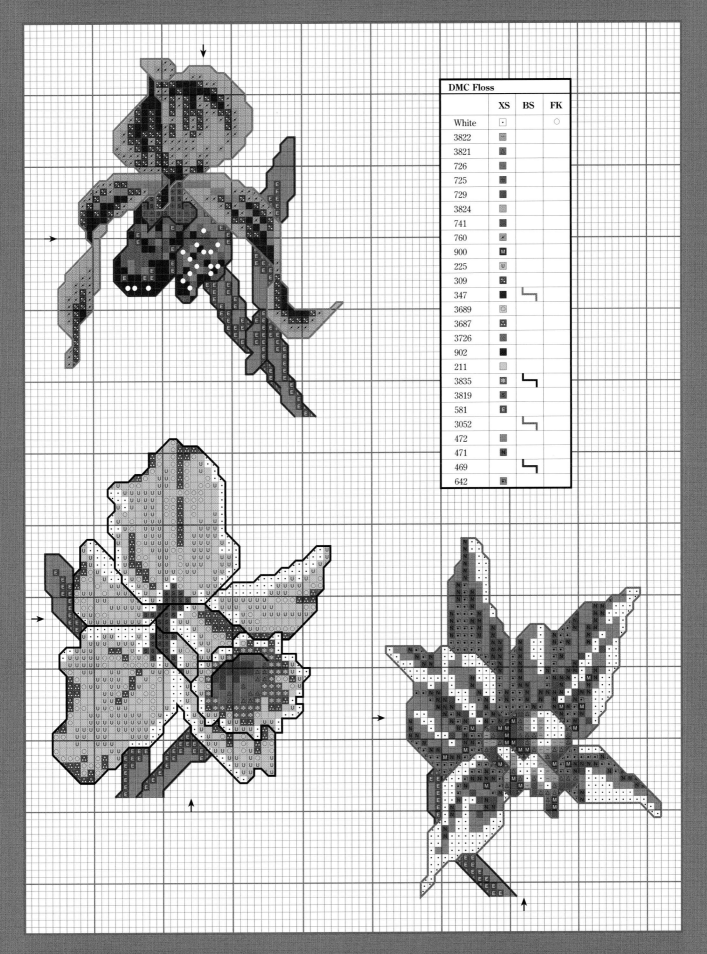

DMC Floss			
	XS	BS	FK
White	·		○
3822	▦		
3821	▲		
726	▦		
725	▦		
729	▦		
3824	▦		
741	▦		
760	◢		
900	M		
225	U		
309	▨		
347	■	⌐	
3689	◎		
3687	▦		
3726	▦		
902	■		
211	▦		
3835	✳	⌐	
3819	S		
581	E		
3052		⌐	
472	▦		
471	N		
469		⌐	
642	▦		

DMC Floss		DMC Floss			
	XS		XS	BS	FK
White	·	3687	▦		
726	■	3803		⌐	
3340	▦	902		⌐	
352	▦	581	E		
351	▦	472	■		●
225		470	▦		
776	✦	469	■	⌐	
962	▦	936	★		
3706	△	935		⌐	
3801	✳	420		⌐	
498	■	355	✚		

Kanji for the word "happiness/joy"

DMC Floss			
	XS	BS	FK
225			
224			●
223			
221			
816		⌐	
814	M		
211			
210			
208			
550		⌐	●
834			
833			

Hold on to your dreams

for each holds

endless possibilities.

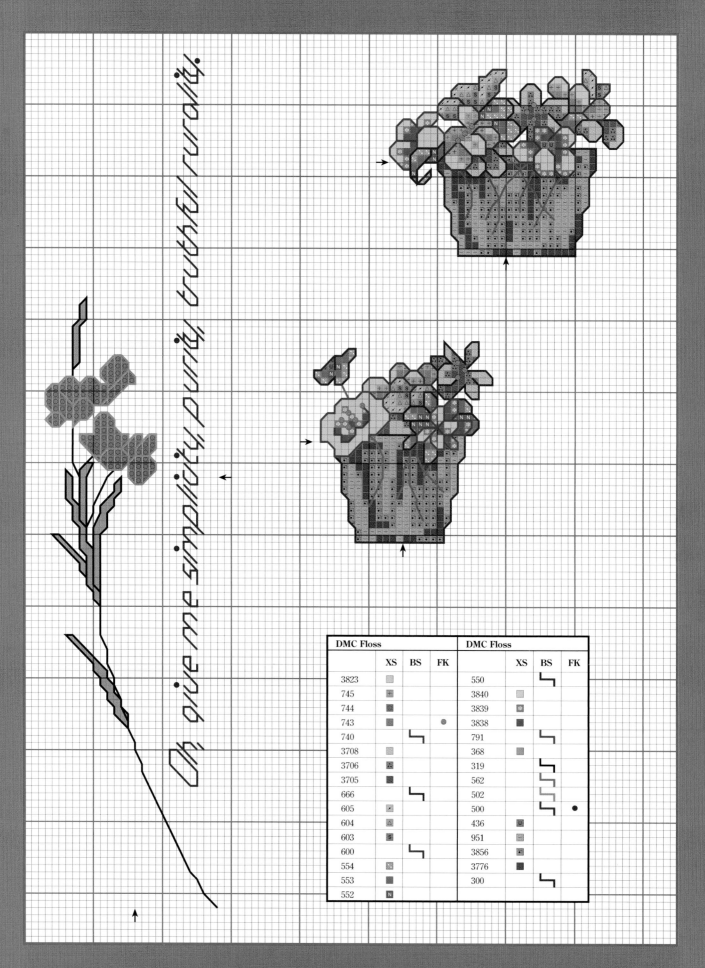

Oh give me simplicity, purity, truthful rurality.

DMC Floss				DMC Floss			
	XS	BS	FK		XS	BS	FK
3823				550		⌐	
745	✛			3840			
744				3839	✳		
743			●	3838			
740		⌐		791		⌐	
3708				368			
3706				319		⌐	
3705				562		⌐	
666		⌐		502		⌐	
605				500		⌐	●
604	△			436	U		
603	S			951			
600		⌐		3856			
554				3776			
553				300		⌐	
552	N						

96

DMC Floss			DMC Floss			DMC Floss			DMC Floss		
	XS			XS	BS		XS	BS		XS	BS
727	▦		720	◙		3688	△		3819	▨	
3821	✳		3777	◼	⌐	815	★		581	E	⌐
3824	▨		351	▨		902		⌐	580		
3341	◉		349	◼		3835	▨		3051	✚	⌐
3340	▨		3689	▢		3834	❋	⌐	3860	▨	

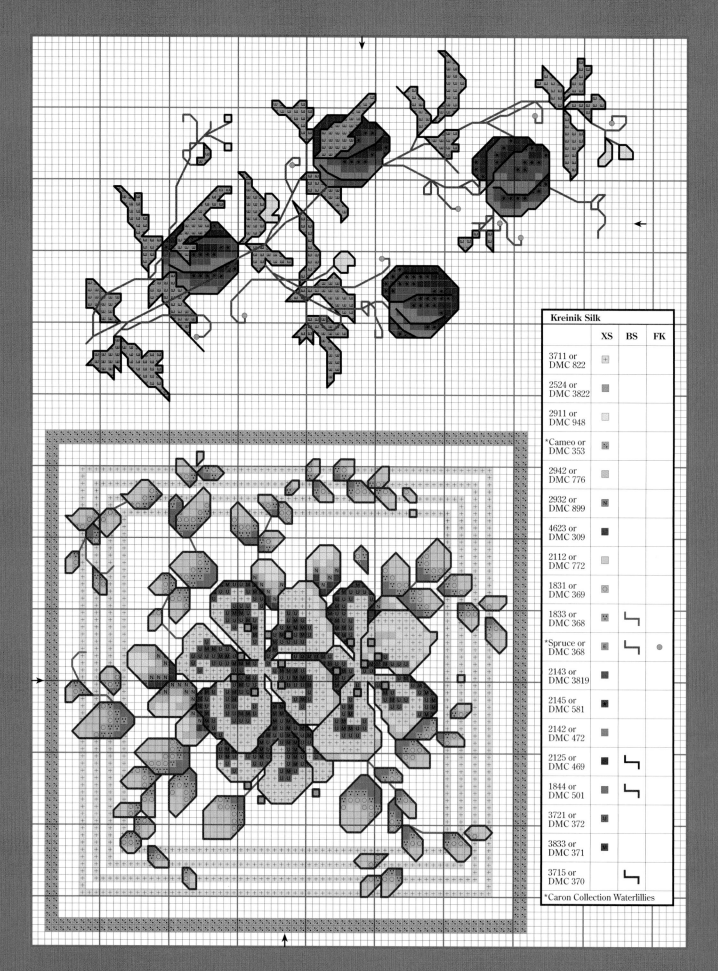

Kreinik Silk			
	XS	**BS**	**FK**
3711 or DMC 822			
2524 or DMC 3822			
2911 or DMC 948			
*Cameo or DMC 353			
2942 or DMC 776			
2932 or DMC 899	N		
4623 or DMC 309			
2112 or DMC 772			
1831 or DMC 369			
1833 or DMC 368		⌐	
*Spruce or DMC 368	E	⌐	●
2143 or DMC 3819			
2145 or DMC 581			
2142 or DMC 472			
2125 or DMC 469		⌐	
1844 or DMC 501		⌐	
3721 or DMC 372			
3833 or DMC 371			
3715 or DMC 370		⌐	
*Caron Collection Waterlillies			

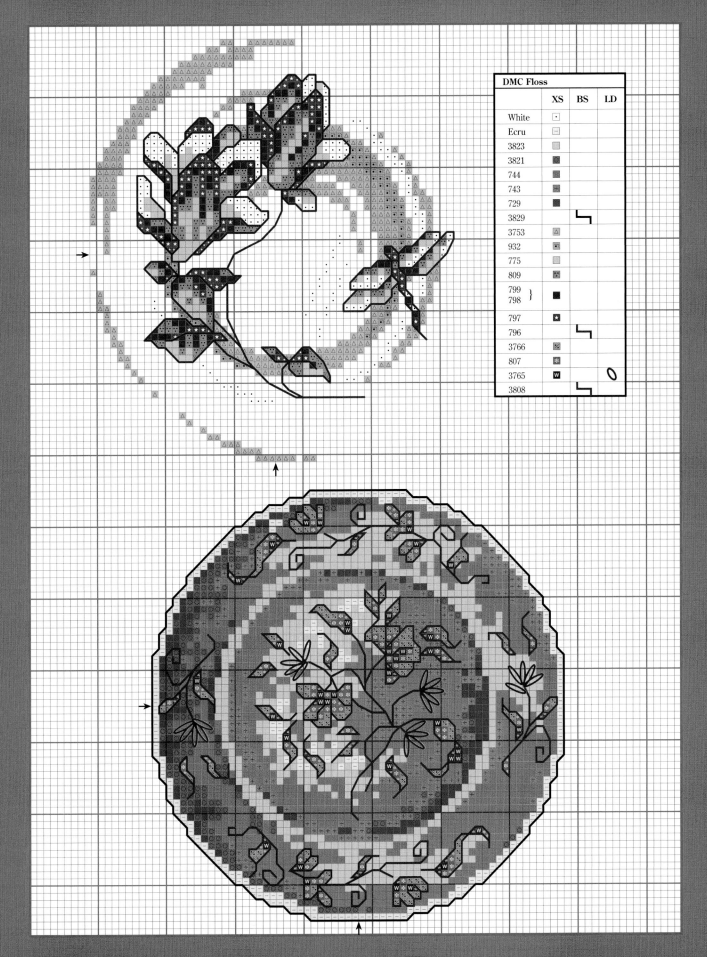

DMC Floss			
	XS	BS	LD
White	·		
Ecru	⊟		
3823	▥		
3821	▨		
744	▦		
743	▤		
729	▦		
3829		⌐	
3753	△		
932	▨		
775	▨		
809	▨		
799 799 798 }	■		
797	★		
796		⌐	
3766	▨		
807	❋		
3765	w	⌐	O
3808		⌐	

European
Fields

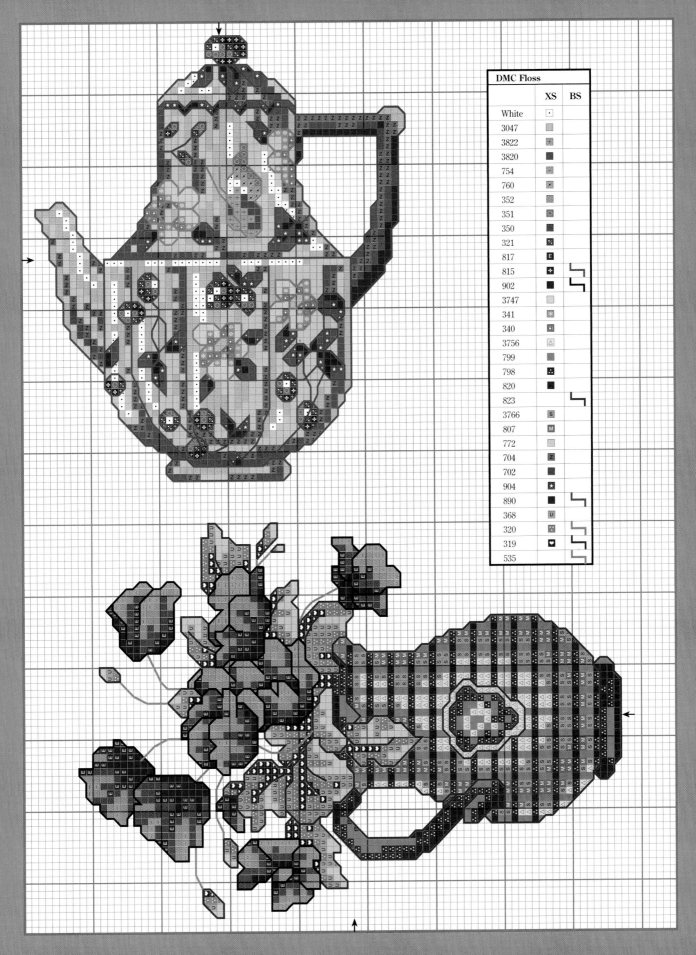

DMC Floss		
	XS	**BS**
White	⊡	
3047	▦	
3822	✦	
3820	▩	
754	▨	
760	▨	
352	▨	
351	◉	
350	▨	
321	▨	
817	E	
815	✚	⌐
902	■	⌐
3747	▨	
341	✳	
340	◧	
3756	△	
799	▨	
798	▨	
820	■	
823		⌐
3766	S	
807	M	
772	▨	
704	Z	
702	▨	
904	★	
890	■	⌐
368	U	
320	▨	⌐
319	♥	⌐
535		⌐

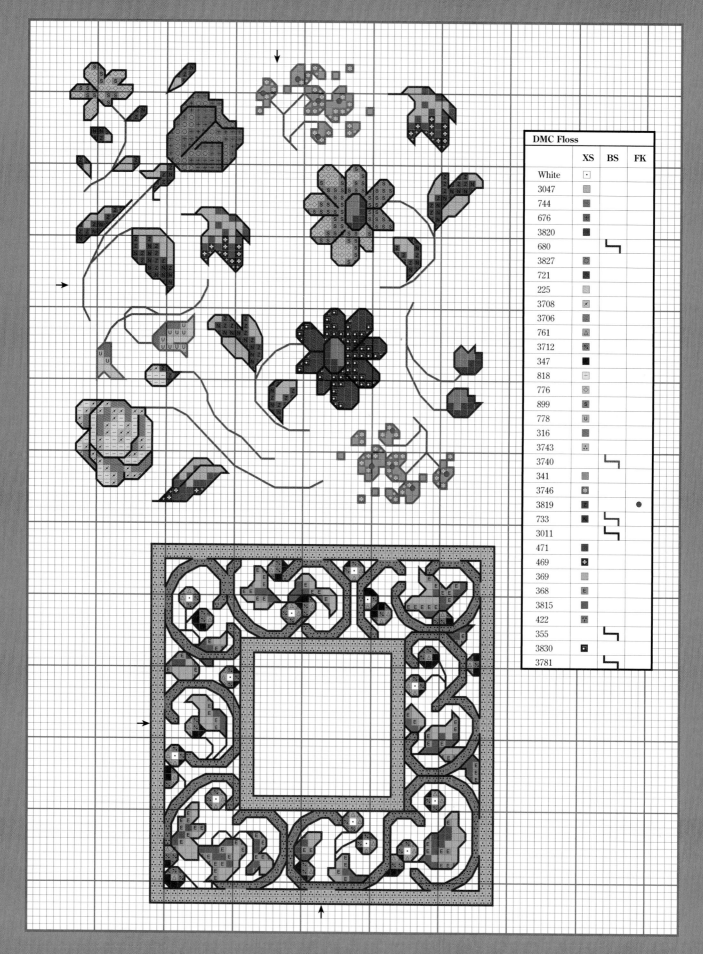

DMC Floss			
	XS	BS	FK
White	·		
3047			
744			
676			
3820			
680		⌐	
3827			
721			
225			
3708			
3706			
761	△		
3712			
347			
818	−		
776	◇		
899	S		
778	U		
316			
3743			
3740		⌐	
341			
3746			
3819	Z		●
733	N	⌐	
3011		⌐	
471			
469	✚		
369			
368	E		
3815			
422			
355		⌐	
3830			
3781		⌐	

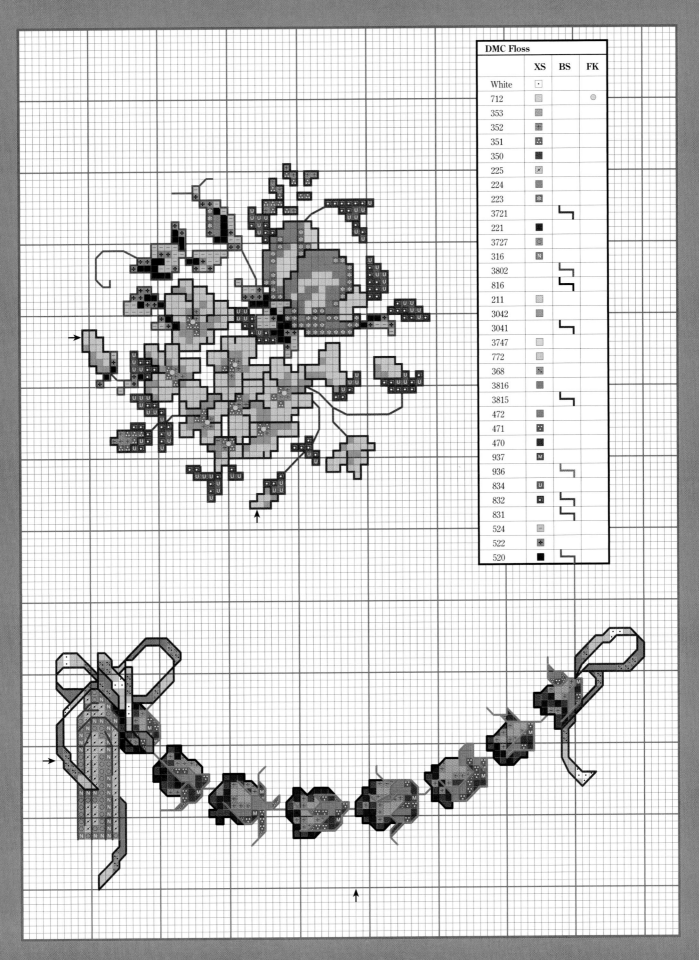

DMC Floss			
	XS	BS	FK
White	·		
712			○
353			
352	+		
351			
350			
225			
224			
223	✳		
3721		⌐	
221			
3727	◎		
316	N		
3802		⌐	
816		⌐	
211			
3042			
3041		⌐	
3747			
772			
368			
3816			
3815		⌐	
472			
471			
470			
937	M		
936		⌐	
834	U		
832	·	⌐	
831		⌐	
524	⊟		
522			
520		⌐	

DMC Floss			
	XS	BS	FK
White	·		
745			
677			
3821			
3829		⌐	
680			
754			
3824			
3340			
352			
351			
3712		⌐	
818	–		
776	U		
223	Z		
3726		⌐	
3721		⌐	●
221		⌐	
211			
209			
3817			
3816			
472	△		
470	E		
936			
3051		⌐	
520		⌐	
834	N		
832			
831			
356	M		
422	S		
420	K	⌐	

104

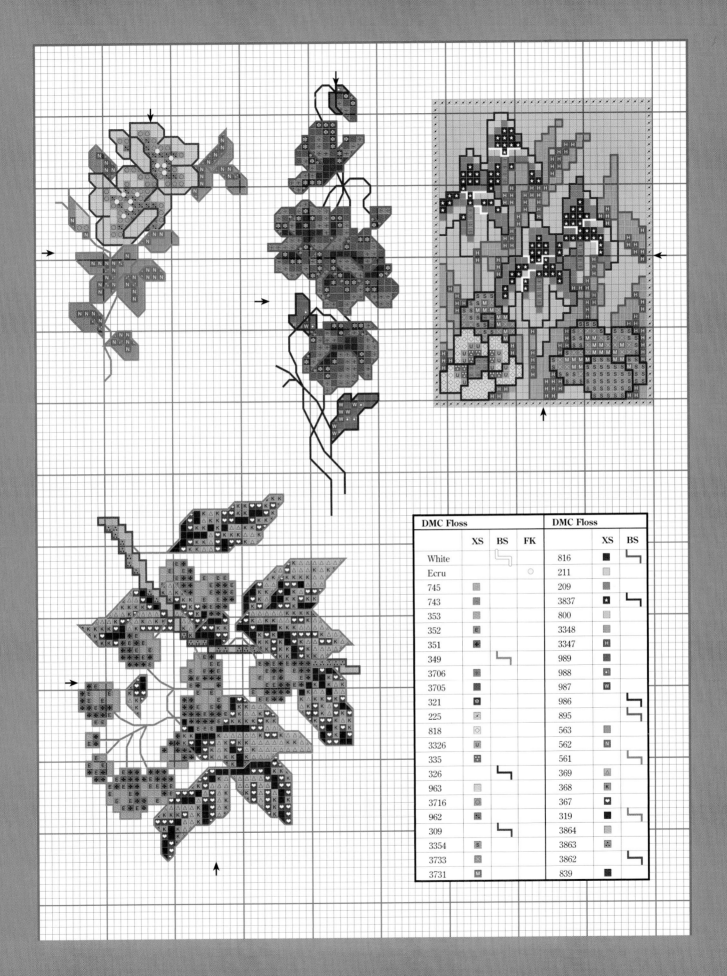

DMC Floss				DMC Floss		
	XS	BS	FK		XS	BS
White		⌐		816	■	⌐
Ecru			○	211	▨	
745	▨			209	▨	
743	▨			3837	★	⌐
353	▨			800	▨	
352	E			3348	▨	
351	✳			3347	H	
349		⌐		989	▨	
3706	▨			988	▣	
3705	■			987	W	
321	✳			986		⌐
225	▪			895		⌐
818	◌			563	▨	
3326	U			562	N	
335	✱			561		⌐
326		⌐		369	△	
963	▨			368	K	
3716	◎			367	♥	
962	✱			319	■	⌐
309		⌐		3864	▨	
3354	S			3863	▨	
3733	✕			3862		⌐
3731	M			839	▨	

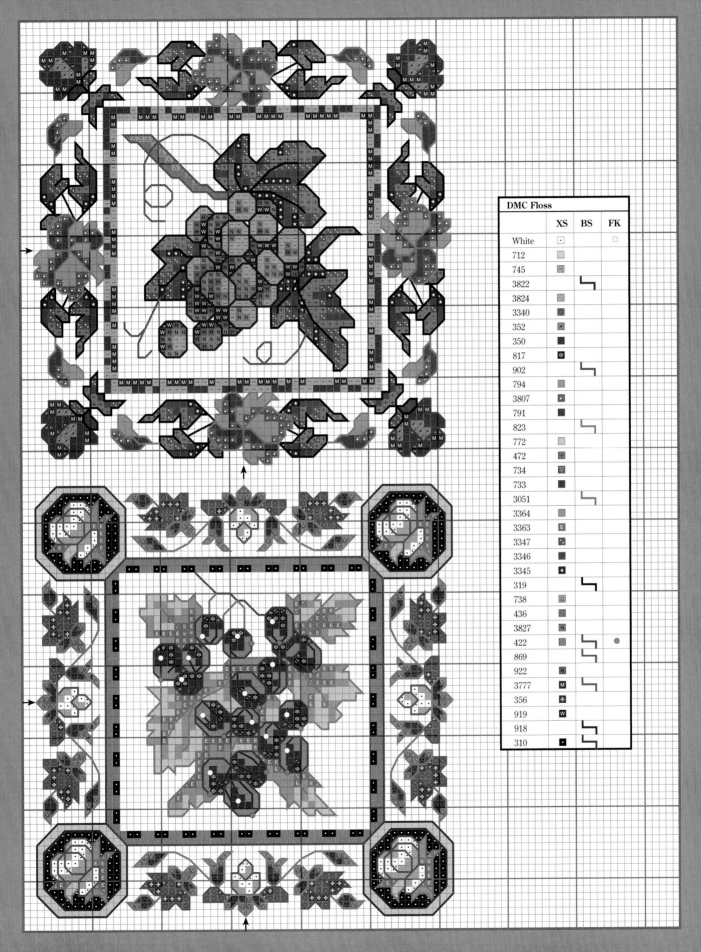

DMC Floss			
	XS	BS	FK
White	·		○
712			
745			
3822		⌐	
3824			
3340			
352			
350			
817			
902		⌐	
794			
3807			
791			
823		⌐	
772			
472			
734			
733			
3051		⌐	
3364			
3363	E		
3347			
3346			
3345			
319		⌐	
738	△		
436			
3827	N		
422		⌐	●
869		⌐	
922	H		
3777	M	⌐	
356			
919	W		
918		⌐	
310	■	⌐	

DMC Floss		
	XS	BS
White	·	
712		
727		
754		
760		
352		
350		
817	❋	
316		
902		⌐
3747		
341		
327		⌐
3348		
3347		
367		
319		⌐
739		
738		
422		
420		
869		⌐

DMC Floss			
	XS	BS	FK
Ecru	⊡		
712	▦		
3047	◪		
3822	⊞		●
3820	▨		
950	Ц		
3779	Z		
3778	▧		
761	▨		
760	◎		
352	A		
350	▨		
817	✳		
224	H		
223	▨	⌐	●
902	■	⌐	
3041	▣		
734	▨		
733	K		
732	✚	⌐	
730	▨	⌐	
834	S	⌐	
832	▨	⌐	
830	W		
739	◈		
738	N		
420		⌐	
356	E		
355	★		

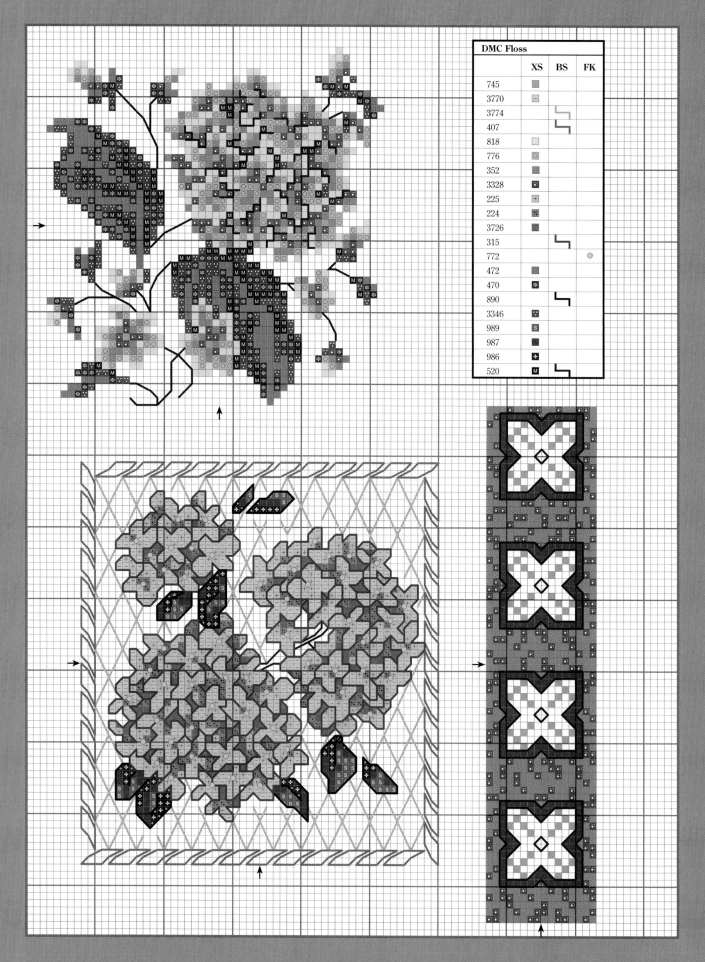

DMC Floss			
	XS	BS	FK
745			
3770			
3774			
407			
818			
776			
352			
3328			
225			
224			
3726			
315			
772			
472			
470			
890			
3346			
989			
987			
986			
520			

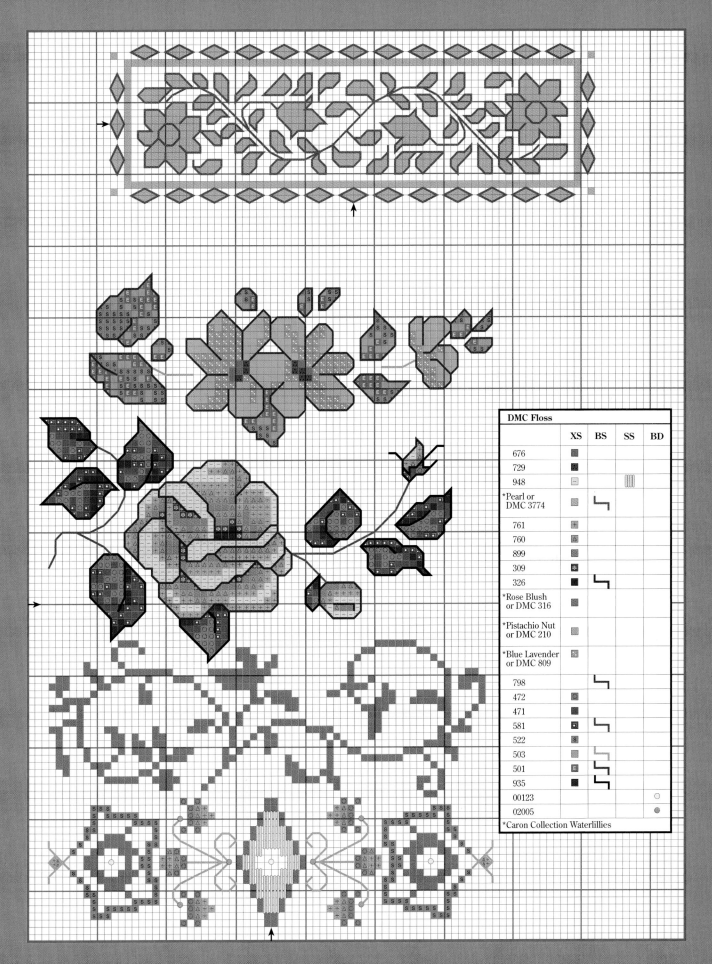

DMC Floss				
	XS	**BS**	**SS**	**BD**
676	▨			
729	▨			
948	⊟		⦀	
*Pearl or DMC 3774	▨	⌐		
761	⊞			
760	▨			
899	▨			
309	✳			
326	■	⌐		
*Rose Blush or DMC 316	▨			
*Pistachio Nut or DMC 210	▨			
*Blue Lavender or DMC 809	▨			
798		⌐		
472	◉			
471	▪			
581	▫	⌐		
522	S			
503	▢		⌐	
501	E		⌐	
935	■		⌐	
00123				○
02005				●
*Caron Collection Waterlillies				

111

DMC Floss		
	XS	BS
712		
744		
726		
3820		
783		
781		
3326		
335	◎	
326		
3609	△	
3607		
814		
211		
341		
340		
3746	M	
828		
792		
791		
772		
3364		
3363		
3362		
368	Z	
367		
3817	U	
3816	N	
500	★	
520		
437		
435	W	
3782		
839		

DMC Floss			
	XS	BS	FK
Ecru	⊟		
712			○
445	▥		
727	▧		
676	▦		
680	■		
760	▨		
899	▩		
309	▦		
3687	▨		
3685		⌐	
778	▵		
316	▨		
3726	▣		
3802	M	⌐	
3819	▨		
581	▦		
580	✳		
369	▦		
320	N		
520		⌐	
833	Z		
3781	✚		
739	✕		
738	U		
3778	E		
355	★		
3031		⌐	●
310	▪		●

113

DMC Floss	XS	FK
712	⊟	●
745	▒	
743	▨	
3046		●
948	▫	
353	▦	
352	▨	

DMC Floss	XS
350	◎
3731	E
3350	▪
3689	△
3688	▨
3687	▣

DMC Floss	XS	BS	FK	LS
3803		⌐		
902		⌐		＼
734				＼
834	▨			
472	▪		●	
471	S			

DMC Floss	XS	BS	LS
470	✳	⌐	＼
469	▪	⌐	
936		⌐	
3348	◎	⌐	
3346	Z	⌐	
3345	★	⌐	

DMC Floss	XS	BS
739	U	
977	N	
976		⌐
3778	▨	
3777	M	⌐
355	■	⌐

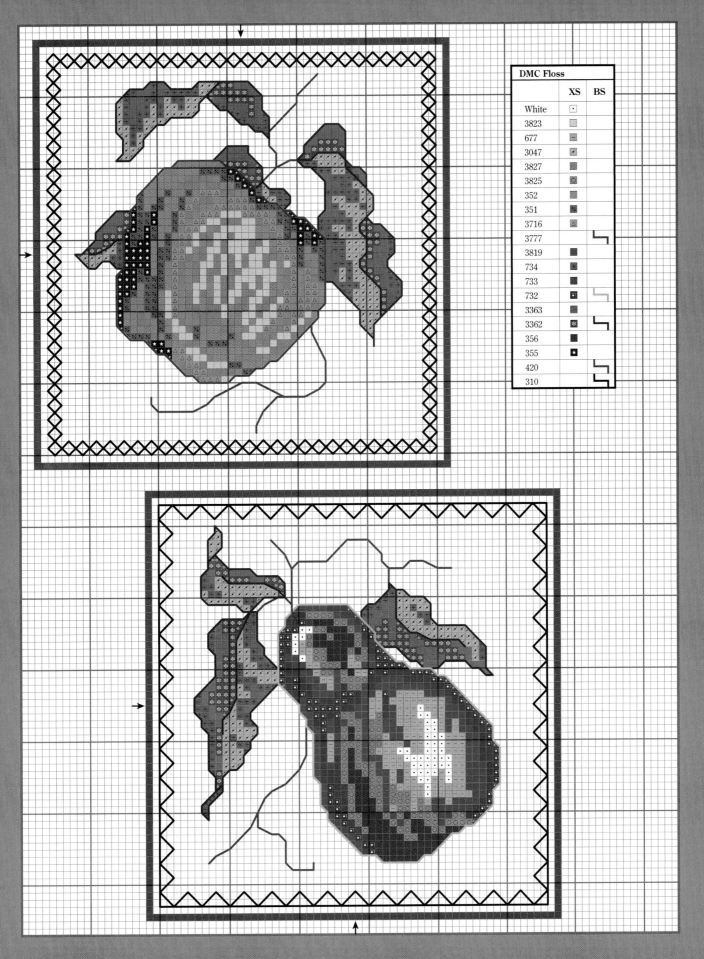

DMC Floss		
	XS	BS
White	·	
3823		
677		
3047		
3827		
3825		
352		
351		
3716		
3777		
3819		
734		
733		
732		
3363		
3362		
356		
355		
420		
310		

DMC Floss		
	XS	
746		
677		
819		
3689	△	
3688		
3687		
917		
915		
814	★	
926		
3819		
581		
580		
472		
471	S	
471 (1 strand)		
3347		
3051	M	
523		
3363	E	
3362		
367		

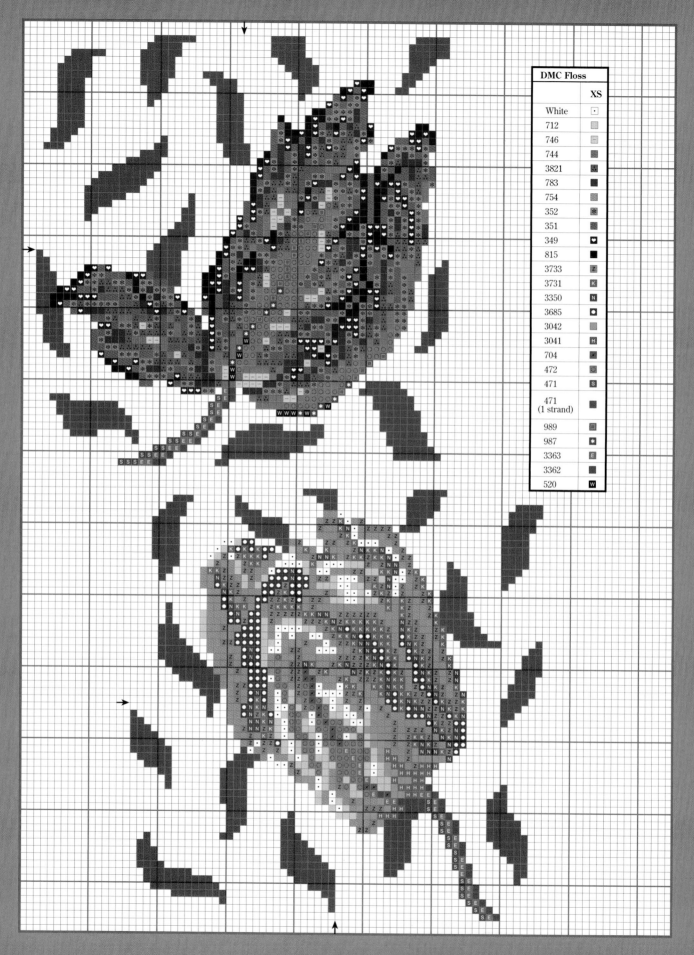

DMC Floss	
	XS
White	·
712	
746	
744	
3821	
783	
754	
352	✳
351	✳
349	♥
815	■
3733	Z
3731	K
3350	N
3685	O
3042	
3041	H
704	
472	◎
471	S
471 (1 strand)	
989	⊞
987	✳
3363	E
3362	■
520	W

DMC Floss			
	XS	BS	FK
White	·		
315		⌐	
211	+		
210	◎		
3743	⊡		
3042	▨		
3740		⌐	
3747	▢		
3348	⊡		●
522		⌐	
472	⊡		
471	■		
470	⊡		
937	✛		
934	■	⌐	
3782	△		
610		⌐	●
3072	▢		
648	▨		
647	S		
646	★		
844		⌐	

DMC Floss				DMC Floss		
	XS	BS			XS	BS
712				210		
3823				208	Z	
745				3740		
744				3364		⌐
726				3362		
676				471		⌐
729				890		
783				966		
780				501		⌐
680				3777	E	
760				433	W	
351				3790		⌐
349				839		
3687	N			3072		
3803				647		
902		⌐				

DMC Floss		
	XS	BS
761		
760		
3712		
347		
815		
800		
799		
798		
797		
820		

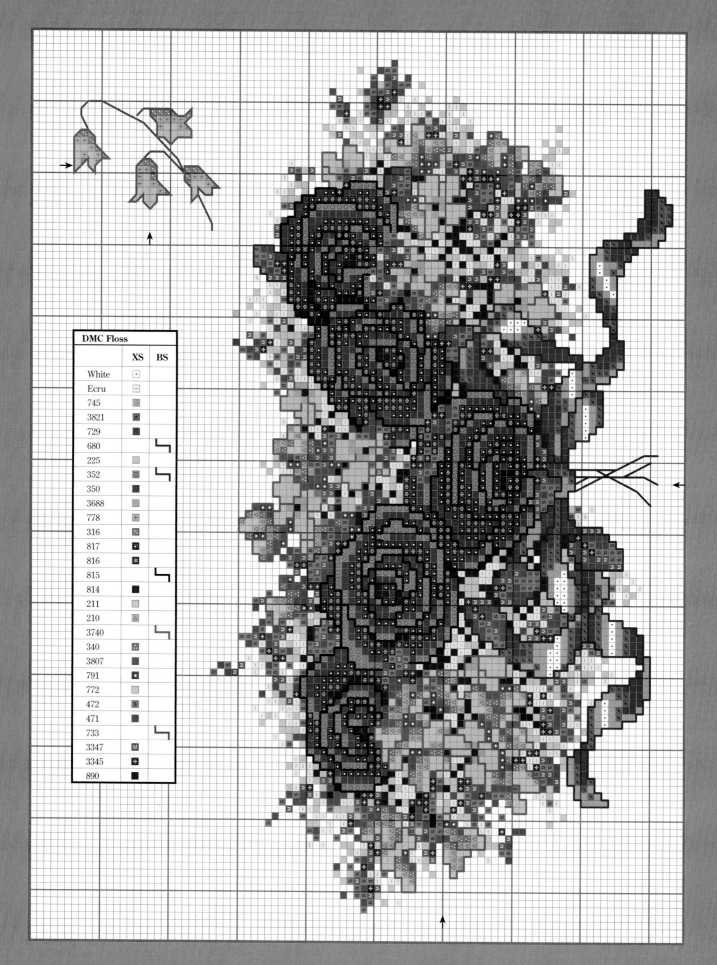

DMC Floss		
	XS	**BS**
White	·	
Ecru	−	
745	▦	
3821	▨	
729	▦	
680		⌐
225	▦	
352	◉	⌐
350	▦	
3688	▦	
778	⊞	
316	▨	
817	▣	
816	▩	
815		⌐
814	▪	
211	▦	
210	△	
3740		⌐
340	▨	
3807	▦	
791	★	
772	▦	
472	S	
471	▦	
733		⌐
3347	M	
3345	✚	
890	▪	

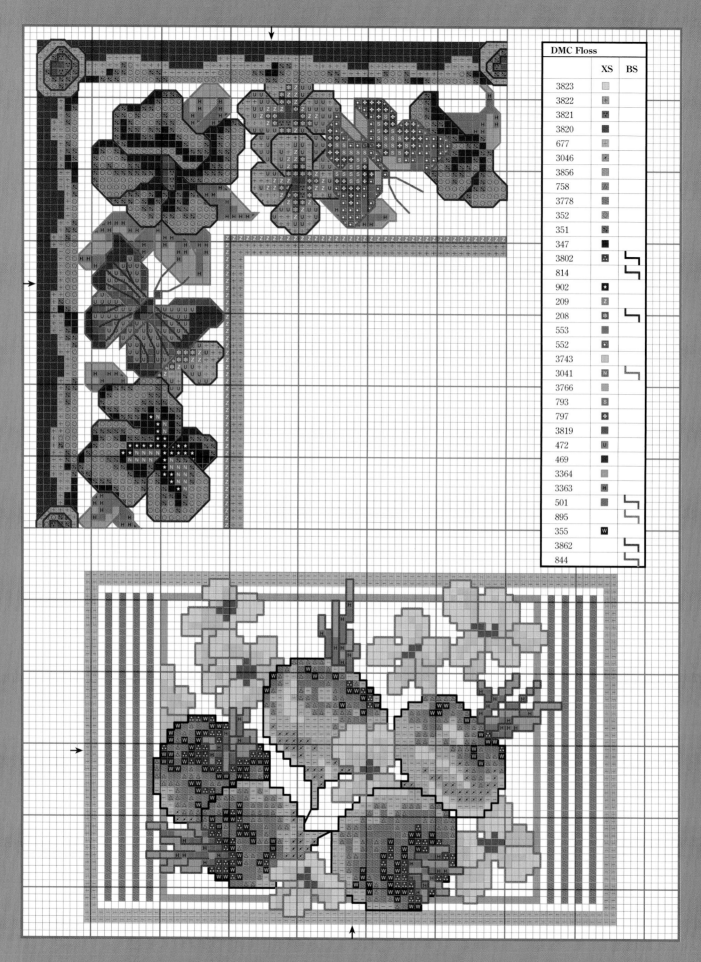

DMC Floss		
	XS	BS
3823		
3822		
3821		
3820		
677		
3046		
3856		
758		
3778		
352		
351		
347		
3802		
814		
902		
209		
208		
553		
552		
3743		
3041		
3766		
793		
797		
3819		
472		
469		
3364		
3363		
501		
895		
355		
3862		
844		

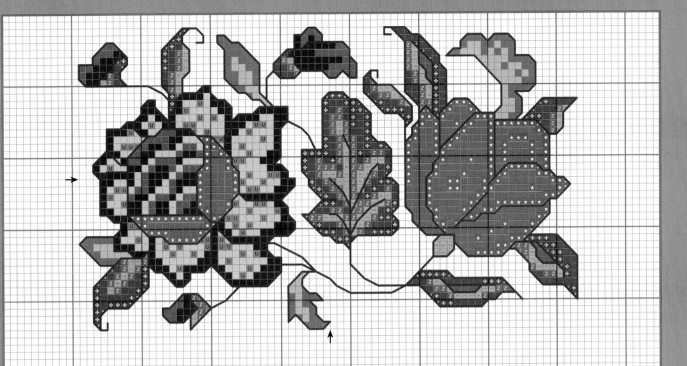

DMC Floss				DMC Floss			
	XS	BS	FK		XS	BS	TR/AW
712				3819			
677				581			
3821				580		⌐	
3820 } *028			●	472	U		
				936		⌐	
680		⌐		734	Z		
948	⊠			733			
722				732			
353				3817			
352				501			
350	S			3810			
349	■			918	M		
817				310		⌐	
902		⌐		13010/ 00283			●
932							
931		⌐					
*Kreinik Blending Filament							

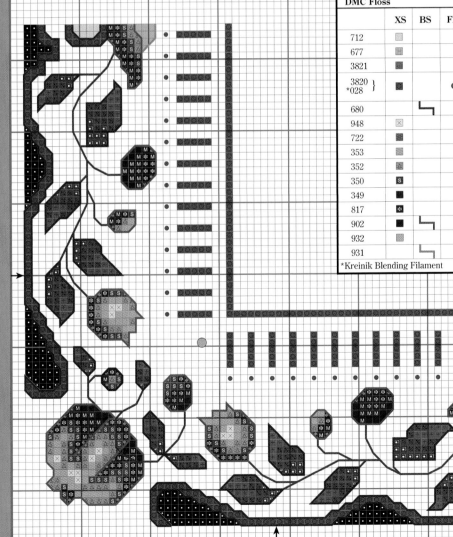

Anchor Conversion Chart

DMC	Anchor	DMC	Anchor	DMC	Anchor	DMC	Anchor	DMC	Anchor
B5200	1	368	214	553	98	722	323	807	168
White	2	369	1043	554	95	725	305	809	130
Ecru	387	370	888	561	212	726	295	813	161
208	110	371	887	562	210	727	293	814	45
209	109	372	887	563	208	729	890	815	44
210	108	400	351	564	206	730	845	816	43
211	342	402	1047	580	924	731	281	817	13
221	897	407	914	581	281	732	281	818	23
223	895	413	236	597	1064	733	280	819	271
224	893	414	235	598	1062	734	279	820	134
225	1026	415	398	600	59	738	361	822	390
300	352	420	374	601	63	739	366	823	152
301	1049	422	372	602	57	740	316	824	164
304	19	433	358	603	62	741	304	825	162
307	289	434	310	604	55	742	303	826	161
309	42	435	365	605	1094	743	302	827	160
310	403	436	363	606	334	744	301	828	9159
311	148	437	362	608	330	745	300	829	906
312	979	444	291	610	889	746	275	830	277
315	1019	445	288	611	898	747	158	831	277
316	1017	451	233	612	832	754	1012	832	907
317	400	452	232	613	831	758	9575	833	874
318	235	453	231	632	936	760	1022	834	874
319	1044	469	267	640	393	761	1021	838	1088
320	215	470	266	642	392	762	234	839	1086
321	47	471	265	644	391	772	259	840	1084
322	978	472	253	645	273	775	128	841	1082
326	59	498	1005	646	8581	776	24	842	1080
327	101	500	683	647	1040	778	968	844	1041
333	119	501	878	648	900	780	309	869	375
334	977	502	877	666	46	781	308	890	218
335	40	503	876	676	891	782	308	891	35
336	150	504	206	677	361	783	307	892	33
340	118	517	162	680	901	791	178	893	27
341	117	518	1039	699	923	792	941	894	26
347	1025	519	1038	700	228	793	176	895	1044
349	13	520	862	701	227	794	175	898	380
350	11	522	860	702	226	796	133	899	38
351	10	523	859	703	238	797	132	900	333
352	9	524	858	704	256	798	146	902	897
353	8	535	401	712	926	799	145	904	258
355	1014	543	933	718	88	800	144	905	257
356	1013	550	101	720	325	801	359	906	256
367	216	552	99	721	324	806	169	907	255

DMC	Anchor	DMC	Anchor	DMC	Anchor	DMC	Anchor	Variegated Colors	
909	923	971	316	3348	264	3776	1048		
910	230	972	298	3350	77	3777	1015	48	1207
911	205	973	290	3354	74	3778	1013	51	1220
912	209	975	357	3362	263	3779	868	52	1209
913	204	976	1001	3363	262	3781	1050	53	——
915	1029	977	1002	3364	261	3782	388	57	1203
917	89	986	246	3371	382	3787	904	61	1218
918	341	987	244	3607	87	3790	904	62	1201
919	340	988	243	3608	86	3799	236	67	1212
920	1004	989	242	3609	85	3801	1098	69	1218
921	1003	991	1076	3685	1028	3802	1019	75	1206
922	1003	992	1072	3687	68	3803	69	90	1217
924	851	993	1070	3688	75	3804	63	91	1211
926	850	995	410	3689	49	3805	62	92	1215
927	849	996	433	3705	35	3806	62	93	1210
928	274	3011	856	3706	33	3807	122	94	1216
930	1035	3012	855	3708	31	3808	1068	95	1209
931	1034	3013	853	3712	1023	3809	1066	99	1204
932	1033	3021	905	3713	1020	3810	1066	101	1213
934	862	3022	8581	3716	25	3811	1060	102	1209
935	861	3023	899	3721	896	3812	188	103	1210
936	846	3024	388	3722	1027	3813	875	104	1217
937	268	3031	905	3726	1018	3814	1074	105	1218
938	381	3032	898	3727	1016	3815	877	106	1203
939	152	3033	387	3731	76	3816	876	107	1203
943	189	3041	871	3733	75	3817	875	108	1220
945	881	3042	870	3740	872	3818	923	111	1218
946	332	3045	888	3743	869	3819	278	112	1201
947	330	3046	887	3746	1030	3820	306	113	1210
948	1011	3047	852	3747	120	3821	305	114	1213
950	4146	3051	845	3750	1036	3822	295	115	1206
951	1010	3052	844	3752	1032	3823	386	121	1210
954	203	3053	843	3753	1031	3824	8	122	1215
955	203	3064	883	3755	140	3825	323	123	——
956	40	3072	397	3756	1037	3826	1049	124	1210
957	50	3078	292	3760	162	3827	311	125	1213
958	187	3325	129	3761	928	3828	373	126	1209
959	186	3326	36	3765	170	3829	901		
961	76	3328	1024	3766	167	3830	5975		
962	75	3340	329	3768	779				
963	23	3341	328	3770	1009				
964	185	3345	268	3772	1007				
966	240	3346	267	3773	1008				
970	925	3347	266	3774	778				

Metric Conversion Chart

mm-millimetres cm-centimetres
inches to millimetres and centimetres

inches	mm	cm	inches	cm	inches	cm
⅛	3	0.3	9	22.9	30	76.2
¼	6	0.6	10	25.4	31	78.7
⅜	10	1.0	11	27.9	32	81.3
½	13	1.3	12	30.5	33	83.8
⅝	16	1.6	13	33.0	34	86.4
¾	19	1.9	14	35.6	35	88.9
⅞	22	2.2	15	38.1	36	91.4
1	25	2.5	16	40.6	37	94.0
1¼	32	3.2	17	43.2	38	96.5
1½	38	3.8	18	45.7	39	99.1
1¾	44	4.4	19	48.3	40	101.6
2	51	5.1	20	50.8	41	104.1
2½	64	6.4	21	53.3	42	106.7
3	76	7.6	22	55.9	43	109.2
3½	89	8.9	23	58.4	44	111.8
4	102	10.2	24	61.0	45	114.3
4½	114	11.4	25	63.5	46	116.8
5	127	12.7	26	66.0	47	119.4
6	152	15.2	27	68.6	48	121.9
7	178	17.8	28	71.1	49	124.5
8	203	20.3	29	73.7	50	127.0

Index